# Racism and Class Struggle

To Sister and
Brother
Hamiltons

'Come ~~do~~ all
Night

Richard

Previously Published

*The American Revolution:*
*Pages from a Negro Worker's Notebook*

# Racism
# and the Class Struggle

## Further Pages from
## a Black Worker's Notebook
## James Boggs

New York and London

Library of Congress Catalog Card Number: 74-105314

First Printing

Monthly Review Press
116 West 14th Street, New York, N.Y. 10011
33/37 Moreland Street, London, E.C. 1

Manufactured in the United States of America

"The Meaning of the Black Revolt in the U.S.A." first appeared in *Revolution*, No. 9, 1963.

"The Black Revolt and the American Revolution" first appeared as "The Black Revolt" in *Monthly Review*, January 1964.

"Liberalism, Marxism, and Black Political Power" first appeared as "Black Political Power" in *Monthly Review*, March 1963.

"Integration and Democracy: Two Myths That Have Failed" first appeared in *Black America*, Fall 1964.

"The City Is the Black Man's Land" first appeared in *Monthly Review*, April 1966.

"Black Power: A Scientific Concept Whose Time Has Come" first appeared in English in two issues of *Liberator*, April and May 1967.

"Culture and Black Power" first appeared as "Power! Black Power!" in *Liberator*, January 1967.

"The Basic Issues and the State of the Nation" was a speech delivered in November 1967. It was first published as "The Final Confrontation" in *Liberator*, March 1968.

"The Future Belongs to the Dispossessed," "The Labor Movement: Revolutionary or——," "Civil Rights Legislation," and "King, Malcolm, and the Future of the Black Revolution" all appeared in slightly modified form as Part III of the Italian edition of *Lotta di classe e razzismo* (Class Struggle and Racism), 1968.

"Democracy: Capitalism's Last Battle-Cry" first appeared as the introduction to the Italian edition of *The American Revolution: Pages from a Negro Worker's Notebook*, 1968.

"The Myth and Irrationality of Black Capitalism" was a speech delivered to the National Black Economic Conference in April 1969.

"Uprooting Racism and Racists in the United States" was a paper prepared for the Frederick Douglass Journalism Fellows, Washington, D.C., October 1969.

# Contents

# Preface

The articles in this book were not written for all time but for our time.

It is not easy to write about a revolutionary movement while it is developing, particularly when it has gained sufficient momentum to bring the counter-revolution onto the scene. The most informative books on revolution are usually those written after the event, when the strategy and tactics, the intrigues and counter-intrigues, the weaknesses and strengths of the revolutionary and counter-revolutionary forces can be laid bare without any fear of endangering the movement. A revolution is not a picnic. It is full of agony and frustration, hate and love, anxiety and fears, violence and death, setbacks and retreats. All these are in a revolutionary movement because it embodies not only the hopes but also the concrete and urgent needs of those in the movement.

Each of these articles was written for a particular audience at a particular time during the course of the last seven years, from 1963 to 1970. The year each was written is given at the end of the article. For example, the first one, "The Meaning of the Black Revolt," was written in 1963 for a world audience which has been and is still confused about the similarities and differences between the black revolt in the United States and the world revolution taking place in Africa, Asia, and Latin America. On the other hand, "Liberalism, Marxism, and Black Political Power," also published in 1963, is a critique of a view of the black revolt which is still widespread among American liberals and Marxists. "The Myth and Irrationality of Black Capitalism," a speech delivered six years later, in 1969, was addressed to an

7

all-black audience, including every segment of the black community, which was just beginning to tackle the fundamental questions of economic development. The concluding essay, "The American Revolution: Putting Politics in Command," was written especially for this volume.

Under these circumstances, there is unavoidably some repetition in the different articles. But this repetition also reflects the complexity of the black revolt in the United States and the need to emphasize and re-emphasize certain critical points.

My wife, Grace Lee Boggs, and I have spent many hours preparing this material over the past few years. We have always been careful to make our projections and appraisals in such a way as to advance rather than impede the movement; yet we believe that we who have had a long life in relation to this and other movements owe the youth of today the benefit of whatever experience and knowledge we have gained along the way.

We have long since learned that no one can predict when or whether a revolution will succeed, but we do know that once the conflicting forces have become as highly developed and as sharply polarized as they are in the United States today, there is no turning back until one or the other side is defeated.

If we are still around when our side has won, then we hope to share with you, the young rebels of today, the responsibilities which belong to the victors. Then, too, we may be able to write a little more about the revolution. If, on the other hand, we falter along the way, we have every confidence that what you will accomplish will be more than we had even imagined would be possible.

—JAMES BOGGS

*Detroit, Michigan*
*January 15, 1970*

# 1

# The Meaning
# of the Black Revolt in the
# U.S.A.

What is happening in South Africa is not too difficult for most people all over the world to understand. In that country the white minority, controlling the government, legally discriminates against and segregates the African majority. The only solution is a revolution by the African majority. The uniqueness of the United States, however, is that, legally and constitutionally, everybody is supposed to be equal and to have equal rights. At the same time, because it is generally understood that the United States is a capitalist country, it is also generally assumed that the black and white workers should be able to find common ground on which to unite and fight against their oppressors. European radicals and those who derive their theoretical inspiration from European radicalism are the ones who particularly assume this. What they fail to recognize is the unique historical development which has created a social structure unique to the United States.

The European powers, through their super-exploitation of the colonial peoples, were able to advance themselves both economically and politically. Not only did the European peoples enjoy material benefits at the expense of the colonial peoples. Such democracy as they enjoyed, on the parliamentary level and on the class struggle level, would never have been possible had it not been for the super-exploitation of the colonies. Nevertheless, by and large the members of the European working class remained in the working class because the super-exploited peoples were outside the mother country.

On the other hand, the United States is the only colonial country in the world which fought a war for independence from

9

the mother country and did not free its slaves; then, eighty years later, fought an internal civil war which allegedly freed these slaves, but having allegedly freed them, systematically set them aside on the basis of race, as an under-class from whose super-exploitation the rest of the population could benefit. No other country can claim or boast this distinction.

Thus within its borders the United States has had its own colony to be exploited by every other segment of the population, economically, socially, and politically. In order to justify this exploitation, the results of which can be seen every day in the stark contrast between the life, work, and rights of blacks and the life, work, and rights of whites, the American people became racists. In order to reassure themselves day after day, year after year, decade after decade, that they were the melting pot of the world where all cultures and races had an equal opportunity to merge—when this was obviously not true—they had to believe that the only reason why the Negroes continued to remain out-casts from the American way of life was because they were racially inferior. Thus when we deal with the American phi-losophy of race relations, we must realize that we are not dealing with ignorance or accumulated prejudice, but with a racist phi-losophy that has been created by the privileges of the rest of the population.

The slogan "black and white, unite and fight," which is ex-plicitly or implicitly accepted by so many liberals and radicals, is based on the erroneous idea that there has been a working-class unity between the races in North American history. The fact is that the white workers have been gaining at the expense of the Negroes for so long that for them to unite with the Negroes would be like cutting their own throats. After the Negroes were set aside to be systematically exploited, every white immigrant who walked off the gangplank to make his way in America was walking onto the Negroes' backs. The classless society of which Americans are so proud is the society in which white workers have been able to climb on the backs of others out of the working class into the middle class. This back-climbing has only been possible because there has always been a Negro under-class at the bottom of society to take the leavings of the jobs, homes, schools, public buildings, etc., as technological development and economic expansion created better opportunities for the whites. It made no difference how much education or how much ability a Negro had compared to a white man. All he could get was the menial job of porter or elevator operator; all he could live in were the buildings which had been abandoned as too old and too dilapidated for the white man. Meanwhile, the white man was moving on to the better jobs, the better schools, the newer homes, that represent progress and the American "way of life." He could only do so because there was a Negro under-class to whom he could bequeath the jobs, the schools, the homes, that the white man considered beneath him.

Thus the American Dream has been a reality for the white man only; it has been a nightmare for the black man. Even after the CIO accepted black workers into the union during the 1930's, the pattern remained. Inside the plant the black workers still do the catch-all jobs—janitor, foundry worker, material handler, etc. —which the white workers consider beneath them. The white workers still exclude the black workers from the skilled jobs which would give them equality inside production. In the union itself, the "place" job of Recording Secretary is in most cases the only one which Negroes are allowed to win.

In the years following World War II, supposedly years of "progress" for the Negro, this exploitation of black workers by white workers has been particularly clear in the growth of the suburbs. For example, following the Detroit riots in 1943 it became impossible to keep black workers from moving out of the oldest buildings in the downtown area and buying homes in white neighborhoods. So the white workers sold their old homes to the Negroes at prices far higher than they had originally paid and at high interest rates, and used the proceeds to buy or build themselves new up-to-date homes and new up-to-date schools in the suburbs.

This is the way the American system has operated, and it has operated in this way as systematically as the imperialist system of exploitation of the colonies has operated.

As long as the Negro struggle for equality remained in the South, it was not easy to recognize that it is a struggle against the actual operation of the American system. The struggle in the South has centered around democratic rights in social and political spheres, such as the right to equal access to schools, to public accommodations, to register, and to vote. It was only following the Birmingham riots in the spring of 1963 that it became possible to see clearly that the enemy of the black revolution is not just the Southern racist but the whole system by which the United States operates.

Birmingham is the Pittsburgh of the South. It is the most highly industrialized city in the South and is most similar to a Northern city in its work and residential patterns. Inside the basic industries the black workers do the dirtiest and hardest work, work which the white workers consider beneath them. Inside the central city the Negro masses live in the black ghetto. It was these ghetto-ized Negroes who broke through police lines on that memorable day in May 1963. Both the President and the Attorney General immediately recognized and stated that the real problem had now become the danger of explosion from the unemployed Negroes concentrated in the Northern cities. The Birmingham events lit the spark which has since erupted in the struggle by Northern Negroes, in cities like Chicago, New York, and Philadelphia, against *de facto* segregation in jobs, schools, and housing. From the moment *de facto* segregation became the issue, the way in which the American system actually operates also became the issue. And the way it has operated and continues to operate is that this is a "land of opportunity" for whites only because there has always been an under-class of blacks, systematically deprived of hope, systematically deprived of opportunity, systematically deprived of participation in the American Dream.

That is why the black revolution, even though it is not an all-American revolution in the sense that it involves all the Americans who are oppressed, is still an American revolution in the sense that it threatens to wreck the whole system by which the United States has operated. In fact, even though black Americans are a minority in the United States, they represent as great a threat to the American system as the African majority represents to the system in South Africa. Because once the bottom of a system begins to explode, then the whole system is threatened with over-throw. Once those at the bottom of the ladder refuse to stay there, then all those who have been climbing on their backs up the ladder are in danger of losing their place on the ladder. The whole system of climbing up out of your class on the backs, first of the Negroes and then of anyone else whom you can exploit, even members of your family—which is what Americans mean by the "classless society"—is now threatened.

It is on the question of jobs that this threat to the system is most explosive. Until approximately ten years ago the American economy expanded chiefly through the mass use of manpower. That is why it was able to assimilate so many waves of immigrants.

If the black revolt had taken place in the years right after World War II when American industry was still expanding by the expanding use of manpower, it might have been possible for the masses of Negro workers to be assimilated into the American system. But the black revolt did not actually begin until 1955, following the Supreme Court decision on schools which, of course, did not actually desegregate any schools but only freed the Negroes to begin the fight for desegregation.

Meanwhile, a technological revolution of automation and cybernation has been taking place in the United States; its main accomplishment, as of now, has been the systematic elimination of the menial, unskilled, and semi-skilled jobs which have been left to Negroes. There are no jobs in agriculture. The old basic industries no longer need Negroes. Even the white workers are being thrown out of the coal mines, the steel mills, the auto plants. Where then are the Negroes to go as they press for equality? The only places they can go are those places which are filled by white workers. The only way they can progress is at the expense of white workers. But the white worker is not going to permit this to happen without a fight. The white worker may abandon his old home to the black worker; he may abandon the old schoolhouse to the black worker; but the one thing he is not going to abandon to the black worker, at a time when jobs are growing scarcer and scarcer, is his job.

The American worker's job is his stake in the American Dream. He works hard so that he can make the "easy payments" on a car, a TV, a hi-fi, a speedboat. And he is ready to defend his job with the same determination that the United Fruit Company, for example, is ready to defend its property investments in Central America. So the Negro struggle for equality, taking place at a time when there is a general decline in the number of jobs, threatens the white worker with expropriation in much the same way as the colonial struggle for national independence threatens the expropriation of the property of the imperialists.

But what about the poor white workers? What about the unemployed white workers? Isn't it logical to assume that they will join together with the black workers? It may be logical, but there is a big difference between what would happen if you lived in a society of logical people and what is likely to happen when you live in a society of real people with real differences. The real fact is that in the United States the poorest white worker has always had one advantage over the richest black man—his color. The poorer the white worker, the more advantage he has taken of this to keep the black man in his place, so that among the growing number of white workers who fear for their jobs, and in the pockets of poverty that exist all over the United States, there is more racism than ever. The whites blame the Negroes for disturbing their dream of America as a land of opportunity.

Hardly a single white worker has joined in the Negro struggle. The only whites who joined the struggle are those who are economically most secure: college students, professionals, intellectuals—individuals who represent no significant social force. The white workers, on the other hand, are mobilizing themselves to resist the Negroes. Not since the 1930's and the organization of the unions has there been such a mass mobilization among white workers. The working class, aided and abetted by the large numbers of middle-class people who have come from the working class, represents the bulk of the counter-revolutionary force against the Negro revolt. Theoretically, it has always been assumed that it was the power structure of a society which encouraged and promoted the counter-revolution. But in the United States it is not so much what the power structure does that is encouraging the counter-revolution as what the workers themselves are doing. The politicians know this very well. So, both on a national and local level, North as well as South, seeking re-election and sensitive to the racism of their constituents, the most liberal politicians try to avoid identification with the Negro struggle and to concentrate on other issues, such as poverty and unemployment.

Those who hope that black and white will unite and fight and dream of solidarity between them do not realize that whenever the American white workers have struggled or supported a struggle for rights in this country, it has not been a struggle for a cause but a struggle in order to get something for themselves. Whenever whites have made or supported concessions to Negroes, it has not been on the basis of solidarity or unity but for opportunistic reasons, to save their own skins. The white workers of the North supported the Civil War against slavery not because they considered the Negro slaves equal human beings but in order to keep the slave-owning economy of the South from encroaching on the Western lands they wanted to homestead. Lincoln freed the slaves by the Emancipation Proclamation after two years of civil war only because the North was losing and he had to resort to desperate measures to "save the Union." After the Civil War the white workers of the North went their merry opportunistic way, ignoring the infamous deal between the Northern capitalists and the Southern landed aristocracy which permitted the South to keep the Negroes in a state of servitude. The white workers didn't care as long as Northern capital was free to industrialize the North and provide them with jobs, and as long as they could "go West" to homestead.

The white workers who organized the CIO in the 1930's admitted a few Negroes for the same reason that Lincoln freed the slaves—to save the Union. They were afraid that the company might use Negro workers to scab. At the beginning of World War II President Franklin D. Roosevelt, under the threat of a march on Washington, issued Executive Order 8802 which admitted black workers into the war plants because he wanted to save the United States from Hitler and Tojo. Later Truman issued an executive order integrating Negroes into lower echelons of the armed services in order to win the war in Korea so that he could save the U.S.A. from the Communists.

It is this kind of opportunism that has been the pattern of American white behavior, regardless of class, toward the Negro. It is the same kind of opportunism that governs the policy of foreign aid to new nations. This opportunism is what gives validity to the Negroes' assertion that Hitler and Tojo did more for them in a few years than all the American people had done for them in 300 years. Hitler and Tojo created a crisis for the American people. With their backs against the wall, they were forced to give the Negroes the opportunity to work in industry long enough to acquire a certain stability from regular employment and therefore in their family lives.

If the black masses in the United States cannot depend on the white workers as their allies, then whom and what can they depend on?

In the early years of the black revolt, one of the most important factors in advancing the struggle was the knowledge that the colored peoples all over the world were struggling for freedom and independence against the Western imperialists. By identifying themselves with these peoples, black Americans, even though they are a minority in the United States, have been able to act with the confidence that they are part of a world majority. But as the struggle in this country has become sharper—and particularly since 1963, when so many thousand Negro freedom fighters were killed, beaten, and jailed—it has become obvious that the moral strength derived from their fraternity with the world's have-not peoples is not enough. Now black Americans must develop methods of struggle which capitalize on two facts: that although they are a minority in the United States, they are one of the world's largest minorities, bigger than most of the nations of the world; and that they are so organically a part of the way the American system operates that their refusal to play this role can disrupt the system irreparably.

The main strategy of the black revolution must be based upon an unrelenting offensive, knowing that if they turn back or slow down, white Americans will have no hesitation in massacring them. Negoes in the South have always known this. That is why it took them so long to begin the struggle. Now this is becoming equally true in the North because as far as the economy is concerned, the Negroes are just as expendable as the Jews were in Nazi Germany.

When it comes to the unrelenting offensive of the Negroes, the white liberal is just as hostile as the white reactionary. The chief reason is that he is afraid that the Negro offensive will increase the anger and antagonism of the white workers and he has enough of an idea of the racism of the white workers to know that it can bring on waves of fascist terror. The Negroes, on the other hand, have no choice but to risk conflict and clashes with white workers, particularly on the question of jobs, because in our society the only measure of income and of social prestige is the holding of a good job. Thus the more Negro workers clash with white workers, particularly on the question of jobs, the more the American people as a whole will have to face the fundamental question posed by the black revolution's coming at the same time as the technological revolution: Why is it necessary to exploit any workers at all when we have machines to exploit?

Now that the black revolution has begun there are only two alternatives for the United States of America. Either the black revolution will succeed, in which case the whole system by which North America operates will be changed and the foundations of a new society—call it what you will—will be laid. Or it will be crushed, and then all Americans will have an opportunity to live under the kind of fascist terror which the black American has had to live under all these years. In either case America will never be the same again.

Neither the average Negro nor the average white realizes that what is at stake in the black revolt is the system. But in what great revolution have the masses on either side realized this? What is really at stake is usually appreciated only by the power structure. In the United States the power structure has so far been content to play the role of peacemaker, trying to make the system work, trying to avoid the crises and confrontations of opposing forces. Thus the Administration, following the Birmingham demonstrations, has advocated civil rights legislation to take the struggle out of the streets.

Negro freedom fighters have been confining the struggle within the framework of the system, but each time the struggle reaches an explosive pitch, more Negroes are driven to recognize that the things they are fighting for cannot be achieved within the system but are rather the ingredients for creating another system.

American capitalism is today the citadel of world capitalism. All over the world, whenever a capitalist government is in crisis or when a European power is forced to yield independence to a former colony, it is the United States which must fill the vacuum, rushing in to control the economy and the politics in order to stave off a revolt which might create a new system and thus threaten the world power of U.S. capitalism. Whenever a new nation gains its independence, the economy and the government with which it is left were originally created as adjuncts to imperialism. It therefore immediately faces the need to create a new economic and political system in order to meet the social needs of the masses of that country.

The Negro revolt helps us to see that essentially the same law is operating inside the present crisis of American democracy. The Negro revolt exposes the whole American system as it has operated in regard to every sphere of the relations between human beings. Coming in the United States at a time when there is no longer any problem of material scarcity, the Negro revolt is therefore not just a narrow struggle over material necessities. It does not belong to the period of struggle over goods and for the development of the productive forces which we can call the era of "Dialectical Materialism." Rather it ushers in the era of "Dialectical Humanism," when the burning question is how to create the kind of human responsibility in the distribution of material abundance that will allow everyone to enjoy and create the values of humanity.

*1963*

# 2
# The Black Revolt
# and the
# American Revolution

I am here to speak to you about the American Revolution that as of now is primarily a Black Revolution. I want to say right here that in the American Revolution, as in every great revolution, it is the issues and grievances, as well as what the counter-revolution does or will do, which will decide where the revolution will go—not any particular insight on my part or on the part of any individual. As I say in my book *The American Revolution:**

> Sometimes the revolution is started by its opponents who by some act arouse the masses to anger and action. Sometimes a very marked improvement in living conditions inculcates in the masses a belief that there is no limit to what they should or can have. Sometimes it is just seeing one segment of the population living so much better than the rest.

Now I did not come here to comfort you. I came here to disturb you. I did not come here to pacify you. I came here to antagonize you. I did not come here to talk to you about love. I came here to talk to you about conflict.

I say this at the outset because the American people have lived for so long under the illusion that America is an exception to the deep crises that rack other countries, that they are totally unprepared to face the brutish realities of the present crisis and the dangers that threaten them. The American people have lived so long with the myth that the United States is a Christian, capitalist, free, democratic nation that can do no wrong, that the

---

* *The American Revolution: Pages from a Negro Worker's Notebook* (New York and London: Monthly Review Press, 1963).

19

question of what is right and what is wrong completely evades them.

In every country, at different times in its history, there is an issue, a question that is unique to that country alone. In India it is the caste system. In the United States it is the Negro question.

For the United States is the only country in the world which fought a war for independence and did not free the slaves; then had to fight a civil war to free these same slaves; but then, having freed them, segregated them off to be systematically exploited and degraded on the basis of color. No other country in the world or in history has committed so brutal a crime. Yet the American people can talk about the crimes of fascism, of Communism, etc., and never even mention the fact that the Negroes in the United States have lived under fascism every day of their lives for over 300 years. This is in itself the acid test of integrity which no American can pass.

Here in New York, I understand that the Dutch purchased Manhattan Island from the Indians for $24 and a few barrels of whiskey. Then, a couple of centuries later, the descendants of these same Indians were put by the descendants of these same Dutchmen into reservations—the first concentration camps in history. Now the Negroes who were brought here in chains over a period of a hundred years are rising up in revolt. And the question that faces the American people is whether they are going to stand by and permit these Negroes to be increasingly put into the concentration camps, stockades, snake-pits, that are being prepared for them, North and South. That so many thousands have already been herded into stockades and prisons and it has not disturbed you enough to make you revolt is sufficient reason for me to want to disturb you, to antagonize you.

The issues of the black revolt are fundamentally rooted in the American system itself. That is the basis of antagonism. Those who have supported this system, those who have benefited from this system, those who have not revolted against this system— and that means every white person in the United States, rich, middle class, and working class—except the students who have laid their lives on the line down South—the antagonism of the blacks is against *you*.

The freedom which Americans have enjoyed more than any other people in the world, and which they feel they can still continue to enjoy, is the freedom to evade responsibility. That is the American way of life. That is the corruption of America itself. It is not so much what the power structure does to Americans as what Americans allow the power structure to do to them and to people all over the world. Corrupted by the material abundance of a land of plenty and a land of opportunity, Americans from the start have evaded political, economic, and social responsibility. They have sloughed such responsibility off as politics.

Thus, for most Americans, freedom means the right to material things.

But the black revolt is for much more. It is against a way of life between people. It is against those who haven't cared what happened to other people as long as they got theirs. It is now too late for the American whites to say they love their Negro brothers. What they have to do is face the conditions which have been created by their going their opportunistic way and making what they call progress at the expense of those at the bottom. What they have to do is face the reason why in every lynch mob there were so many Christians and believers in democracy whose hands were reeking with the blood of blacks.

I said in my book that I believed in democracy, but I didn't believe in being too damn democratic. I went on to explain how one can call himself a believer in democracy and still be a hypocrite about every human value of any importance. But the very fact that I raised any question at all about democracy immediately raised questions in people's minds as to what I am *for*. If I am not for democracy, then they suspect that I am for something worse than democracy—fascism, Communism, or some other kind of ism. They can never conceive that there might be something better than democracy.

Let me say here, once and for all, that under this democracy of which Americans are so proud there has been more systematic exploitation of more people than there has been under any other political system. This is the truth which the black revolt is beginning to expose. And as the black revolt proceeds, what it is going to show is that there is another form of society which is much higher than democracy. Because democracy is a system which has benefited the few at the expense of the many. Democracy is a system which has been made possible by the worst kind of class system in the world—the *class* system that is based upon the systematic exploitation of another *race*. The black revolt, on the other hand, if it succeeds, will make possible a classless society. If it doesn't succeed, and that is also possible, then not only Negroes but all Americans will know what it is like to live under fascism.

American democracy is unlike any other democracy in the world. In other Western democracies the people who were super-exploited and kept from progressing in order to make progress possible for the motherland, were the people in the colonies. In the United States, the under-class which was exploited to make progress possible for the dominant race was the native Negro. In other countries the ordinary working people did live much better than the super-exploited people in the colonies. But for the most part they remained in the working class. They still remained at the bottom of the ladder. But in the United States, because there was always an under-class of Negroes kept in place at the bottom of the ladder, the other workers could climb on their backs up the social ladder into the middle class.

Thus American democracy, unlike other democracies, has been that peculiar kind of society where climbing up on the backs of other ordinary persons is valued and cherished as the American way of life. This is what opportunity means in America—the opportunity to climb up on the backs of others. This opportunity, this system of back-climbing, is what the average American boasts about as the "classless society." Actually it is the worst kind of class society in the world because it encourages one group of workers to use another group of workers to climb up on.

If it succeeds, as I said before, the black revolt will get rid of this kind of "classless society" and put in its place a real classless society.

Sometimes a revolution starts because the people believe that the country in its present form can do more for them than it is already doing. So they go out and ask for these things which they call their rights under the system. If they get these rights and don't press for more, then the country has made a social reform. But if they don't get what they believe are their rights and they continue to fight for them, they begin to make a revolution.

In the United States, following the Supreme Court decision of 1954, the Negroes proceeded to do just this. They began demanding rights which they felt the country had admitted were theirs and which many Negroes felt could easily be granted under the Constitution. But in the period since 1954, Negroes have found that every institution in the country, from the Constitution on down, cannot guarantee or give them the rights they are entitled to. The Supreme Court decision, instead of guaranteeing them any rights, has only set them free to *fight* for these rights. To this day no agency of the government—federal, state, or local —has enforced these rights in anything but the most token sense. The Negroes have been left to struggle and to devise means of struggle for themselves. The myth that American democracy protects the rights of Negroes has been exploded.

At the same time that the myth of American democracy as a protector of social and political rights for Negroes has been exploded, a technological revolution of automation and cybernation has been taking place in this country. This technological revolution has brought home to the Negroes the truth about how the *economic system* actually operates under democracy. This technological revolution has brought mass unemployment to Negroes more than to any other group of workers. It has shown how the economic progress of the country and the social progress of other Americans have been made possible only by keeping the Negroes as an under-class at the bottom of the ladder, an unskilled reserve labor force to be super-exploited for the benefit of every other section of American society. It isn't automation which is responsible for mass unemployment of Negroes; it is the *system* of keeping Negroes at the bottom as an under-class, uneducated and unskilled, which is responsible.

Now the Negroes are exploding, tearing up that bottom, refusing to stay in that place at the bottom. That means that everybody who is on top of them on the ladder is likely to fall. And it means also that the very system of climbing up on the backs of others who are kept at the bottom is threatened. That is why the black revolt represents the possibility of a real classless society rather than the kind of classless society which we have had—which was classless or almost classless for whites because the class of whites could stand on top of the under-class of Negroes.

That is the general perspective of where the black revolt is going to end up—if it succeeds. But this perspective, which is on "the other side of the mountain," can only be realized by the harshest, the bitterest, the most brutish conflicts between Negroes and white workers, between the Negroes representing a revolutionary force and the white workers representing a counter-revolutionary force. Because right now—and it will get much worse in the immediate future—there is an absolute decline in the number of jobs due to automation: at least 40,000 jobs are being eliminated each week, two million every year. At the same time two million new workers are coming into the work force every year. Negroes are not going to stop asking for these jobs just because the number of jobs is declining. They are going to keep demanding these jobs because that is the way this system operates. You have to have a job, you have to work in order to live and in order to have social respect. The competition between Negro and white workers for jobs is going to increase in bitterness, in brutishness.

Up to now, most Negroes and also their sympathetic white friends have believed that the Negro struggle was simply a matter of struggling for integration. That is, they have believed that the Negro struggle was a struggle to be assimilated into American society. Now all of them, Negroes and whites, have to face the fundamental facts of the system. They have to face the fact that the capitalist system in America has exploited the working people in its own peculiar way, by separating off one section of workers from the other, one after another, one wave of immigrants after the other, and always with the Negroes at the bottom.

After the system has operated by separation all these years, after the system has made its progress by separating workers and encouraging workers to climb up on top of the backs of other workers, you can't just integrate those who have been separated by the system. You have to change the system. You have to put another kind of system in its place. You have to put another kind of classless society in place of the kind of hypocritical classless society that has exploited the Negroes so systematically and so separately and which they are now revolting against.

So, in conclusion, the black revolt is tearing up the myth of democracy.

It is beginning to tear up the myth of capitalism being the best of all possible systems.

It is beginning to explode the myth that Christianity makes man moral.

Finally, it is going to prove to whites that they have had freedom and opportunity only because they always had someone beneath them to exploit, not only here but in the rest of the world as well.

*1963*

# 3

# Liberalism,
# Marxism,
# and Black Political Power

In *The Negro Revolt*,* Louis Lomax gives a moving historical account of the step-by-step movement of American Negroes into American life: first, their arrival as imported slaves; next, their rise as free men during Reconstruction; and then, as a result of political manipulations both in the national Congress and in the Southern states, the rapid decline of their short-lived freedom until finally, by the end of the nineteenth century, they were not even being treated as well as during the period of slavery. Lomax also points out something that few other writers have bothered to say: that long before 1619, a number of Negroes had come to America, not as slaves with only their naked backs, but as part of the early force of adventurers, playing a role in the settling of the Western hemisphere and bringing with them some of their own culture.

Then, very rapidly, Lomax traces the futile attempts made by Negroes to establish themselves in business with the aim of setting up a black economy. The failure of this effort left them with no alternative but to become wage earners in white industries. Next, as Lomax describes the different organizations that have been formed over the years as weapons for Negro liberation, the book really picks up momentum and one begins to feel the pull of the Negro mass. Not only does Lomax deal seriously with the rise of these organizations and the role that they have played; he also makes a penetrating analysis of why today most of these organizations face the loss of support by Negroes. For either what they seek to achieve is no longer what the Negroes want, or the pace of their achievement is too slow

---

* Louis Lomax, *The Negro Revolt* (New York: Harper & Row, 1962).

for the impatient demands and the pent-up emotions of black men in revolt. If for no other reason than to understand the shifts in the Negroes' support of various organizations and the contradictions and conflicts which are now faced by Negro leaders as they try to find out where the Negro masses are, this book is worth its price.

It is when Lomax tries to do what Negro leaders themselves have not been able to do—that is to say, tries to plot a direction for the Negro struggle and make proposals as to the Negroes' allies in this struggle—that he gets into serious trouble.

The NAACP began as an organization to *defend* Negroes in the period when they couldn't defend themselves, relying mainly upon white courts to give favorable decisions to black men, under laws written and interpreted by white legislators, white judges, and white juries. It began to falter when it could not meet the new challenge of Negroes wanting to go over to the *offensive*. The new organizations, like the Congress of Racial Equality (CORE), the Student Non-Violent Coordinating Committee (SNCC), and Martin Luther King's Southern Christian Leadership Conference (SCLC) have been mainly direct-action groups. They take the law out of the courtroom and begin to implement or test it in action, in the streets and in the market place. This is the stage which the Negro struggle has already reached and from which it cannot retreat.

There is only one apparent exception to this generalization, and it is a most important one: the Black Muslim movement, which the author too lightly dismisses as just a group of fanatics. It would be much closer to the truth to say that the Muslims are in fact planting the ideological seed for the next stage of revolt. The Black Muslims are doing something which no other Negro organization has attempted, rehabilitating Negroes spiritually and morally to the point where they feel that they are men in every sense of the word and are the salt of the earth, and that, being men in every sense of the word and the salt of the earth, what they want is *not* integration with whites, but separation and independence from white society, because they reject white society and all its ways and values. This idea, which Mr. Lomax feels is mumbo-jumbo, is the heart of the Negro question and

*Duality of black struggle*

the American Revolution today. It is through this that we can begin to comprehend the Negro revolt in its present stage in the United States.

The United States was built up on an economy of slavery. That in itself was no crime. Many societies and countries have been based on slavery. The crime of the United States is that it is the first and only country which, having freed its slaves legally, by proclamation, by law and in the courts, then continued to enslave them and deny them equal rights on the basis of their color. The unique character of the Negro question in the United States stems from the infamous raw deal of 1877 which permitted the Southerners to keep the Negroes in servitude as long as the Northern industrialists could industrialize the country and accumulate capital and the white workers could have homesteads in the West to provide the foodstuffs needed for an industrialized East. It is this deal which has given the Negro struggle both its *class* and its *race* character.

In most countries the struggle of the oppressed has been of a class character only. But in the United States the Negroes have not only been at the bottom of the economy, they have been kept there on a race basis. Therefore, it is not just the economic system against which the Negro struggles, as many Marxists would like to have it. And it is not just a question of persuading and re-educating some Southern Bourbons and reactionaries, as the liberals would like to believe. The Negro is kept at the bottom of the economic ladder by another *race* which keeps him there because of *his* race and which benefits from keeping him there. Therefore, all those people above the Negro —i.e., all the whites—become responsible for the Negro's position, either actively or passively. It is not just Big Business or management or the rulers of the economic system who are allied against the Negroes. It is the white *people*. This is what gives the Negro struggle its peculiar duality: it is both a class struggle of the bottom revolting against the very structure of the American system, and also a race struggle because it is directed against the American white people who have kept Negroes at the bottom of their society. The rebellion of the Negroes today, like the slave revolts of the pre-Civil War days, is therefore a revolt, and not just some sort of a "race riot," as the white politicians from Right to Left continue to think of it.

Lomax ends his book by giving reasons why Negroes should stick with the liberals. Behind his reasoning is the assumption that Negroes want exactly what whites have. Lomax never faces the truth behind the common saying among Negroes that all the white man has is his "white." This "white" is exactly what the Negro despises and doesn't want any part of, because it is nothing but racial superiority. So that when a Negro says that the whites have better opportunities, what he means is that these better opportunities exist only in relation to an opportunity that Negroes are denied. Or to put it the other way, when a Negro says that he wants equality of opportunity, what he means is that he wants *a system of equality* or a way of life in which there is no advantage to anyone on the basis of race. Under these conditions, what the whites now have will no longer exist. Only if Negroes wanted to be superior or to look down on another race would they want to be like whites.

Lomax thinks Negroes need the support of white liberals because he envisages the Negro being gradually elevated into white society. He can only see Negroes as a minority who must depend upon these liberal forces. This is a position similar to that held by most Marxists on the Negro question, except that the Marxists substitute the working class for the liberals as the ally that the Negroes need. Neither Lomax, purporting to speak for the liberals, nor the Marxists, purporting to speak for the working class, face the fact that great revolutions have never depended upon sheer numbers but rather upon the relationship of forces in the existing political arena. Today, when the existing political arena is a world arena, the Negro's relationship is to the world. The more revolutionary he and the world become, the more clearly he sees this relationship between himself and the world as part of the revolution that is taking place in the world. As he knows, and as all white America also knows, "the whole world is watching."

Marxists are still thinking of Negroes in terms of their pre-war role as sharecroppers in the countryside. They have not grappled with the new reality of the agricultural revolution in

America and of the Negroes' migration to the big cities and their concentration in the center of these cities.

Both liberals and Marxists are imprisoned in thought patterns that have now become outmoded by the industrial and social development of the past generation. They are still thinking in categories of the democratic revolution at a period when Negroes have become the hub of the industrial centers of the country, and when what Negroes are fighting for is part of the world revolution and therefore against the whole structure of American society. They are looking so hard at the Negroes' color that they can't see the Negroes' social, economic, and world role in relation to the accumulation of capital, to the development of automation, and to the world revolution of the have-nots.

Theoretically, the Marxists are worse than the liberals. The Marxists recognize that a revolution is involved in the Negro struggle but still they want the Negroes to depend upon the white worker being with them. The Negro worker who works in the shop knows that if he is going to depend on the white worker he will never get anywhere. The average white worker today isn't joining any liberal organizations or radical organizations. If he is joining anything, he is joining racist organizations like the Home Improvement (i.e., keep the Negroes out) Associations, the Ku Klux Klan, and the White Citizens' Councils. The white worker is becoming more of an enemy every day. Labor unions, which were supposed to be the most advanced part of America, are to this day practicing and fostering discrimination in the same manner as every other segment of American society. Only recently, at the Chrysler-Jefferson plant where I work, when it was rumored that management was going to promote a few Negroes into skilled trades, it was the steward who rushed to the men to arouse them to protest against Negroes coming into the department. It was not the company's fault, as Marxists would have the Negroes believe. It was the fault of plain American workers. For when the Negro fights, he fights not "in the last analysis"—i.e., not according to the thought patterns of the Marxists—but *in reality*. His enemy is not just a class. His enemy is people, and the people are American whites of all classes, including workers.

The liberals are basing their whole case upon the assumption that Negroes want to integrate into white society and be equal within the present mess. We have to be very clear about this. America has never been based upon equality for all. It has always been based upon equality for a few, with the others trying to climb up on each other's backs so that they could be equal to those at the top and above those at the bottom. Most Negroes in the United States not only know this, they also know that their greatest progress has come when disaster has struck American society rather than when America was flourishing or because of the goodness of the American people. The first real upsurge came with World War I, when thousands and thousands of Negroes flocked to the North. The second upsurge came with World War II, when Negroes were able to work in industry en masse for the first time because of Hitler and Tojo, a fact which leads many Negroes to say today that Hitler and Tojo did more to advance the Negro cause in four years than Americans have done in four hundred. It is by facing this fact that one can begin to grasp that the Negro struggle is in no sense either a struggle to salvage American society or purely an American struggle; rather it is a struggle of an exactly opposite nature.

What is fundamentally wrong with Lomax's book is that it is written by a Negro who still thinks in terms of white power as naturally as he thinks of eating when he's hungry. His mind simply has not stretched beyond the idea of whites ruling and giving Negroes a greater share in this rule. He doesn't visualize that it could be the other way around, that it is in fact time for Negro political power to manifest itself. In the South today the one thing that both Negroes and whites are clear about is that when Negroes think of voting they are thinking of voting for Negroes to replace whites because they know that only when they do that will they get their rights. That is why whites are so determined to keep Negroes from voting. But up North where Negroes have been voting for decades, they still don't know what they are voting for. This is particularly true in the urban centers where Negroes have simply not grappled with what is implicit in the fact that who is mayor and who is police commissioner is decided by where the Negro vote goes. In no major city have the Negroes yet elected a mayor. Nor has any Negro writer yet realized that a Negro mayor of a big city like Detroit or Chicago or Philadelphia would be as natural as an Irish mayor once was in Boston or a white mayor now is in Minneapolis or Las Vegas or some little town in Maine where the whites are the overwhelming majority.

It is only when Lomax can break clear of the image of the Negro always asking the whites for something and can begin thinking of Negroes ruling that his mind will be able to move to where the Negro nationalist organizations have moved. The struggle of the Negroes in the very near future will be the struggle for black political power, and by black political power is meant, not the power of Negroes to put white men in office, to whom they can then go and ask for things, but rather their own power to dispose over things.

*1963*

# 4

# Integration
# and Democracy:
# Two Myths That Have Failed

Myths, superstitions, and folklore have been with us down through the ages and perhaps will always be with us. They have often served a useful purpose because they give emotional feeling to a philosophy. But myths endure much longer than philosophies: people will hold on to a myth even when cold reason tells them that the philosophy no longer has a basis in fact. It is then that what began as a philosophy becomes pure and simple myth, and it is then also that myths become particularly useful to the rulers of a society, whether these be tribal chieftains, feudal lords, or capitalists.

Today in the United States there are two philosophies that have become myths: democracy and integration. The first, democracy, is not unique to the United States. A belief in democracy has been shared by almost all Western nations, and they have at one time or another tried to impose it on the rest of the world. However, integration as a philosophy is unique to the United States because this is the only country which has been built upon the systematic assimilation of successive waves of immigrants into the American—i.e., the capitalist—system. Each of these waves of immigrants was assimilated into the American system by climbing on the backs of others, first and always on the backs of the Negroes, and then on the backs of other immigrants until each reached a status more or less equal to that of the Founding Fathers. The word "integration" was not used to describe this systematic process until the Negroes (who had come here at the same time as the Founding Fathers) began to demand assimilation on the same basis as the immigrant. It

33

was only then that the concept of assimilation began to appear revolutionary, rather than a natural part of the system.

The first thing that every revolutionist has to be clear about is that integration is not in itself a revolutionary concept. It means assimilation into the system rather than a radical transformation of that system on the basis of new values and new methods. The only thing that has made integration seem revolutionary up to now is the way it has been resisted by whites, and particularly by those whites who have most benefited from it—the former immigrants. And it is this resistance which is beginning to reveal the mythical elements in the philosophies of democracy and integration.

Any radical—revolutionist or militant, socialist or otherwise—who in modern-day society thinks of a revolution taking place through the democratic process is propagating myths and illusions and deluding himself and those he claims to lead. There is no question that in fighting for integration the Negroes will have to resort to actions of a revolutionary character. But there is also no question that *if* the Negroes could achieve integration into the American system by the democratic process, that would not be a revolution. A revolution involves the taking away of power—economic, political, and social power—by one section of society (the oppressed) from another section of society (the oppressors).

Up to now most Western Marxists have been frustrating themselves trying to reconcile democracy with revolution. They have wondered, for example, why Castro (who admittedly has the support of the majority of the Cuban people) does not conduct democratic elections. They refuse to face the fact that democratic elections in Cuba would mean encouraging the old ruling classes to seek power, which they could only win with the support of the military forces of imperialism. They also refuse to face the fact that it was the democratic process which created the conditions making the revolution necessary in the first place. It is only by looking at the whole world and seeing all the nations that have been dominated and exploited by the democratic nations that you can begin to examine scientifically whether democracy has been a philosophy for liberating the world or for subjugating the world. And unless you look at democracy in terms of the whole world, you are propagating a myth which is as much a vise around the minds of people as any superstition or folklore has ever been.

Democracy has been used for so long to describe so many different systems that it is only a source of confusion for revolutionists. The capitalists use it, the Communists use it, socialists use it, liberals use it, extremists use it, fascists use it, racists use it. It makes no difference what economic system is involved, what political objectives are at stake, what methods are being employed. The United States is in South Vietnam fighting for democracy; it seeks to overthrow Castro in the name of democracy. Wallace is in Alabama fighting for democracy; and Goldwater is all over America doing the same.

The South Africans are upholding democracy in South Africa. It makes no difference that the United States would never permit the Vietnamese to vote on whether they want the U.S. in Asia, or that the South Africans would never permit the Africans to vote on what kind of government they want. Democracy has been used to obscure and evade issues for so long that the real questions of "how," "why," or "where" a system should be tackled or a crucial issue resolved can no longer be faced.

These confusions and evasions are built into the concept of democracy. The Greeks invented the word to describe equality in the political arena. But Greek democracy did not give political equality to the slaves: it gave no slave the right or the power to free himself from slavery. Instead it rested upon the foundation of slavery. Similarly, Western democracy has rested upon capitalist and imperialist exploitation. And the American democracy of which this country has been so proud has rested upon the worst kind of exploitation of all—a class system of exploitation that is based upon the systematic exploitation of another *race*.

Thus democracy has never been—nor was it ever meant to be—a process by which an exploited people could make a revolution. At its best democracy has been a means whereby minor reforms could be achieved in between revolutions. During these interim periods it has allowed the process of negotiation to take place between opposing sections of society—for example, through unions or civil rights organizations. But it has never been a way of making revolution because a revolution means the taking of power, and the taking of power means confronting the armed forces of the state with the armed forces of the oppressed.

The socialists who say "comes the revolution" so glibly have never faced this question seriously because their perspective is based on the belief that a working class which is constantly growing in numbers and organization in the process of production will be forced to revolt by the agony of the work process and the unequal distribution of material wealth. For years, particularly in the United States, socialists visualized the revolt as coming through the democratic process because of the increasing unity, organization, and control of production by the workers inside the plant. Then, in the 1930's, they witnessed the labor movement taking over the plant but not taking power in the political arena, the only arena where they could control the military and other police forces of the state. Since that time socialists no longer even envisage the revolution in terms of the taking of power. Their policy centers instead around moral persuasion and embarrassment of the powers-that-be, accompanied by a vague hope that some day another Great Depression will cause the poverty-stricken masses to unite and fight again. Thus their perspective for revolution is based more on a catastrophe overtaking the capitalist class than on anything the people will do or could do or should do to take power.

Today few socialists envisage a revolution by the workers of North America or Western Europe. Whether they admit it or not, they know that these workers are the actual prop which supports the counter-revolutionary forces in the United States all over the world. Wherever it goes, whatever it does, whomever it supports, the United States does it to save democracy. The American workers are not ignorant of what this country is doing. Yet they never ask themselves whether the United States is doing what it does by a majority vote of the people in those countries or on the invitation of some puppet minority which wants to preserve its political power, its social privileges, and its economic exploitation of the majority.

Today, whether Negroes realize it or not, as long as they demand integration and democracy they are demanding the right to become capitalist exploiters, first of each other and then, if this is not enough, imperialist exploiters of the underdeveloped world. Yet Negroes should understand this better than any other Americans: For over 300 years they have lived as a semi-colonial people inside a country where democracy has meant racist degradation of anyone colored and class exploitation of anyone poor.

For any socialist or black nationalist to be revolutionary today, he must be for a total change of this society by revolutionary means and the construction of a society which eliminates the exploitation of all other races, classes, and nations which is inseparable from capitalism and democracy. Particularly in the United States, where for the first time in human history a majority is enjoying the material abundance of an affluent society, the revolutionist has to be clear that majority rule does not mean a revolutionary transformation of society but rather the continued repression of the substantial minority through whose super-exploitation this affluent society was built. At this point in particular the revolutionist must grapple with the fact that majority rule *inside* the United States already means full-fledged fascist rule over the peoples of Asia and Latin America, and is leading to full-fledged fascism at home—as reflected in the white backlash majority and the growing retaliation against Negroes, radicals, and liberals who threaten the democratic right of the majority to uninterrupted enjoyment of the fruits of exploitation. Thus majority rule can easily become for all Americans the fascism that the Negro has known all his life.

The role of the revolutionist is not to encourage others to become part of a system. It is to change the whole system. The aim of the revolutionist is not more democracy or more integration. It is to create a system which assures the equal right of all, regardless of race or class or nation, to live as full human beings. Today a revolution has taken place in technology which makes it possible to free man for the first time from the slavery of the work process and the machine and yet provide enough material goods for this country and some of the developing world. Exploitation and domination of classes, races, and nations are no longer necessary and universal citizenship can be a reality. But such a way of life cannot come by voting or by wishing or asking or persuading or praying. It can only come by the revolution.

*1964*

# 5

# The City
# Is the
# Black Man's Land

Population experts predict that by 1970 Afro-Americans will constitute the majority in fifty of the nation's largest cities. In Washington, D.C., and Newark, N.J., Afro-Americans are already a majority. In Detroit, Baltimore, Cleveland, and St. Louis they are one-third or more of the population and in a number of others—Chicago, Philadelphia, Cincinnati, Indianapolis, Oakland —they constitute well over one-fourth. There are more Afro-Americans in New York City than in the entire state of Mississippi. Even where they are not yet a majority, as in Detroit, their school children are now well over 50 percent of the school population.

In accordance with the general philosophy of majority rule and the specific American tradition of ethnic groupings (Irish, Polish, Italian) migrating en masse to the big cities and then taking over the leadership of municipal government, black Americans are next in line. Each previous ethnic grouping achieved first-class citizenship chiefly because its leaders became the cities' leaders, but racism is so deeply imbedded in the American psyche from top to bottom, and from Right to Left, that it cannot even entertain the idea of black political power in the cities. The white power structure, which includes organized labor, resorts to every conceivable strategy to keep itself in power and the black man out: urban renewal or Negro removal; reorganization of local government on a metropolitan area basis; population (birth) control. Meanwhile, since their "taxation without representation" is so flagrant, safe Negroes are

---

* Co-authored with Grace Lee Boggs.

appointed to administrative posts or hand-picked to run for elective office. In Hitler-occupied Europe such safe members of the native population were called collaborators or Quislings.

All these schemes may indefinitely delay or even permanently exclude the black majority from taking over the reins of city government. There is no automatic guarantee that justice will prevail. But those who invent or support such schemes must also reckon with the inevitable consequences: that the accumulated problems of the inner city will become increasingly insoluble and that the city itself will remain the dangerous society, a breeding place of seemingly senseless violence by increasing numbers of black youth, rendered socially unnecessary by the technological revolution of automation and cybernation, policed by a growing occupation army which has been mobilized and empowered to resort to any means considered necessary to safeguard the interests of the absentee landlords, merchants, politicians, and administrators, to whom the city belongs by law but who do not belong in the city and who themselves are afraid to walk its streets.

America has already become the dangerous society. The nation's major cities are becoming police states. There are only two roads open to it. *Either* wholesale extermination of the black population through mass massacres or forced mass migrations onto reservations as with the Indians (White America is apparently not yet ready for this, although the slaughter of thirty-two blacks in Watts by the armed forces of the state demonstrates that this alternative is far from remote.) *Or* self-government of the major cities by the black majority, mobilized behind leaders and organizations of its own creation and prepared to reorganize the structure of city government and city life from top to bottom.

This is the dilemma which Northern liberals have been evading ever since May 1963, when the Birmingham city masses (Birmingham is over 40 percent black) took the center of the stage away from Dr. Martin Luther King and precipitated a long hot summer of demonstrations, followed by a long hot summer of uprisings in Harlem, Philadelphia, Rochester, New York, and New Jersey in 1964. The McCone Commission has warned that the 1965 revolt in Watts may be only a curtain-raiser to future violence in the nation's ghettos unless the public adopts a "revolutionary attitude" toward racial problems in America; and Vice-President Humphrey proclaims that the "biggest battle we're fighting today is not in South Vietnam; the toughest battle is in our cities." But the war is not only *in* America's cities; it is *for* these cities. It is a civil war between black power and white power whose first major battle was fought last August in southern California between 18,000 soldiers and the black people of Watts.

A revolution involves the conquest of state power by oppressed strata of the population. It begins to loom upon the horizon when the oppressed—viewing the authority of those in power as alien, arbitrary, and/or exclusive—begin to challenge this authority. But these challenges may result only in social reform and not in the conquest of power unless there is a fundamental problem involved which can be solved only by the political power of the oppressed.

It is because labor is becoming more and more socially unnecessary in the United States and another form of socially necessary activity must be put in its place that a revolution is the only solution. And it is because Afro-Americans are the ones who have been made most expendable by the technological revolution that the revolution must be a black revolution.

If the black liberation movement had erupted in the 1930's in the period when industry was in urgent need of unskilled and semi-skilled labor, it is barely possible (although unlikely in view of the profound racism of the American working class and the accepted American pattern of mobility up the economic and social ladder on the backs of others) that Afro-Americans might have been integrated into the industrial structure on an equal basis. But the stark truth of the matter is that today, after centuries of systematic segregation and discrimination and only enough education to fit them for the most menial tasks abandoned or considered beneath their dignity by whites, the great majority of black Americans now concentrated in the cities cannot be integrated into the advanced industrial structure of America except on the most minimal token basis. Instead, what expanding employment there has been for Afro-Americans has been in the fields of education and social and public service (teaching, hospitals, sanitation, transportation, public health, recreation, social welfare). It is precisely these areas which are the responsibility of city government, and it is also precisely these areas of activity which are socially most necessary in the cybercultural era. But because the American racist tradition demands the emasculation of blacks not only on the economic and sexual but also on the political level, the perspective of black self-government in the cities cannot be posed openly and frankly as a profession and perspective toward which black youth should aspire and for which they should begin preparing themselves from childhood. Instead, at every juncture, even when concessions are being made, white America makes clear that the power to make concessions remains in white hands. The result is increasing hopelessness and desperation on the part of black youth, evidenced in the rising rate of school dropouts, dope addiction, and indiscriminate violence. Born into the age of abundance and technological miracles, these youths have little respect for their parents who continue to slave for "the man," and none for the social workers, teachers, and officials who harangue them about educating themselves for antediluvian jobs.

The fundamental problem of the transformation of human activity in advanced America is as deeply rooted as the problem of land reform in countries which have been kept in a state of underdevelopment by colonialism. Like the colored peoples of the underdeveloped (i.e., super-exploited) countries, Afro-Americans have been kept in a state of underemployment, doing tasks which are already technologically outmoded. But where 75 to 80 percent of the population in a country like China or Vietnam lives in the countryside, a comparable proportion of Afro-Americans now lives in the cityside. And whereas countries like China or Vietnam still have to make the industrial revolution (i.e., mechanize agriculture and industry), North America has already completed this revolution and is on the eve of the cybercultural revolution. Socially necessary activity for the majority in an underdeveloped country is essentially industrial labor; education for the majority is vocational education. The peasantry has to be educated to the need to abandon outmoded farming methods, prepare itself for technological change, and meanwhile be mobilized to work to provide the necessary capital for modern machinery. It can be educated and mobilized for this gigantic change only through its own government. In an advanced country like the United States, on the other hand, the black population, concentrated in the cities, has to be educated and mobilized to abandon outmoded methods of labor and prepare itself for the socially necessary activities of political and community organization, social services, education, and other forms of establishing human relations between man and man. As in the case of the underdeveloped countries, this can be achieved only under its own political leadership. Hence the futility of the War on Poverty program, which is essentially a program to keep the poor out of the *political* arena where the controlling decisions are made and to train them for industrial tasks which are fast becoming as obsolete in advanced North America as farming with a stick already is in Asia, Africa, and Latin America.

Marcus Garvey and Elijah Muhammad, the only two leaders who ever built mass organizations among urban blacks, both recognized the need for self-government if the Afro-American was ever to become a whole man. Both of them seemed to understand intuitively Aristotle's dictum that "man is a political animal." Garvey created a political apparatus and proposed a "Back to Africa" program which to many seemed fantastic. It was difficult for him to do otherwise in the period after World War I when Negroes were making their first mass migration to the big cities from the agricultural hinterland but had not yet reached sufficient numbers or development for him to envisage their political leadership of the cities. Muhammad's strength has also been in Northern cities. His most pronounced achievement, the rehabilitation of black men and women, was based on his philosophy that the so-called Negro would inevitably rule his own land, and his creation of an organizational framework (The Nation of Islam) which approximates the structure of government, including leaders, followers, taxation, discipline, and enforcement agencies. Muhammad's weakness was his failure to recognize the significance of technological development in an advanced country; hence his concentration on land ownership and small businesses. Also, as so often happens with those who build a powerful organization, he became preoccupied with the protection of the organization from destruction by a determined enemy. As a result, when the Northern movement erupted in 1963, he did not take the offensive which, consciously or unconsciously, large numbers of non-Muslim blacks (the so-called 80 percent Muslims) had been hoping he would take. It was this failure to take the offensive which led to Malcolm X's split from the organization. That such a split was inevitable was already portended in Malcolm's now-famous speech to the Northern Negro Grassroots Leadership Conference in Detroit on November 10, 1963, in which he analyzed the black revolution as requiring a conquest of power in the tradition of the French Revolution and the Russian Revolution. Malcolm was assassinated before he could organize a cadre based on his advanced political ideas, but in one of his last speeches he made very clear his conviction that "Harlem is ours! All the Harlems are ours!"

It was in 1965 that black militants began to discuss Black Power seriously. Before 1965 the movement had been so dominated by the concept of integration, or the belief that the "revolution" would be accomplished if American Negroes could win equal opportunities to get jobs, housing, and education, that even those black militants who were profoundly opposed to the American way of life devoted a major part of their time and energies to the civil rights struggle. What, up until 1965, few black militants had grappled with is the fact that *jobs* and *positions* are what *boys* ask to be *given*, but *power* is something that *men* have to take and the taking of power requires the development of a revolutionary organization, a revolutionary program for the reorganization of society, and a revolutionary strategy for the conquest of power.

As early as August 1963, at the March on Washington, the idea of Black Power had been anticipated in John Lewis's speech threatening to create another source of power, and in the announcement of the formation of a Freedom Now Party by William Worthy. In 1964 the Freedom Now Party won a place on the ballot in the state of Michigan and conducted a state-wide campaign running candidates for every state-wide office and stressing the need for independent black political action. The party did not win many votes, but it contributed to establishing the idea of independent black political power inside the Northern freedom movement. In early 1965 a Federation for Independent Political Action was created in New York by militant black leaders from all over the country who went back into their communities to link the idea of black power with concrete struggles. On May 1, 1965, a national Organization for Black Power was formed in Detroit.

The first task which the Organization for Black Power set itself was to establish a scientific basis for the perspective of Black Political Power in the historical development of the United States. Thus, the following statement was adopted at the founding conference:

At this juncture in history the system itself cannot, will not, resolve the problems that have been created by centuries of exploitation of black people. It remains for the Negro struggle not only to change the system but to arrive at the kind of social system fitting to our time and in relation to the development of this country.

That Negroes constitute this revolutionary social force, imbued with these issues and grievances that go to the heart of the system, is not by accident but a result of the way in which America developed. The Negroes today play the role that the agricultural workers played in bringing about social reform in agriculture and the role that the workers played in the 1930's in bringing about social reform in industry.

Today the Negro masses in the city are outside of the political, economic, and social structure, but they constitute a large force inside the city and particularly concentrated in the black ghettos.

The city itself cannot resolve the problems of the ghetto and/or the problems of the city. The traditional historical process by which other ethnic groupings were assimilated into the economic and political structure has terminated with the arrival of the Negroes en masse (1) because of the traditional racism of this country which excludes Negroes from taking municipal power as other ethnic groupings have done; and (2) because of the technological revolution which has now made the unskilled labor of the Negroes socially unnecessary. The civil rights movement which originated in the South cannot address itself to these problems of the Northern ghetto which are based not upon legal (*de jure*) contradictions but upon systematic (*de facto*) contradictions. It remains therefore for the movement in the North to carry the struggle to the enemy in fact, i.e., toward the system rather than just *de jure* toward new legislation.

At this conference we arrived at the recognition that the prop, the force, that keeps the system going is the police which is an occupation force of absentee landlords, merchants, politicians, and managers, located in the city, and particularly in the black ghetto, to contain us.

Negroes are the major source of the pay that goes to police, judges, mayors, common councilmen, and all city government employees, taxed through traffic tickets, assessments, etc. Yet in every major city Negroes have little or no representation in city government. WE PAY FOR THESE OFFICIALS. WE SHOULD RUN THEM.

The city is the base which we must organize as the factories were organized in the 1930's. We must struggle to control, to govern the cities, as workers struggled to control and govern the factories of the 1930's.

To do this we must be clear that power means a program to come to power by all the means through which new social forces have come to power in the past.

1. We must organize a cadre who will function in the cities as the labor organizers of the 1930's functioned in and around the factories.

2. We must choose our own issues around which to mobilize the mass and immobilize the enemy.

3. We must prepare ourselves to be ready for what the masses themselves do spontaneously as they explode against the enemy—in most cases, the police—and be ready to take political power wherever possible.

4. We must find a way to finance our movement ourselves.

Since the founding conference, and particularly since the Watts revolt and the deepening crisis from the U.S. occupation of Vietnam, black revolutionaries all over the country have been working out the theory and practice of building a black revolutionary organization.

1. They are clarifying what black political power would

mean in real terms, that is to say, the program which black government in the cities would institute. Thus, for example, Black Political Power would institute a crash program to utilize the most advanced technology to free people from all forms of manual labor. It would also take immediate steps to transform the concept of welfare to one of human dignity or of well-faring and well-being. The idea of people faring well off the fruits of advanced technology and the labors of past generations without the necessity to work for a living must become as normal as the idea of organized labor has become. There should be no illusion that this can be accomplished without expropriating those now owning and controlling our economy. It could not therefore be accomplished simply on a city-wide basis, i.e., without defeating the national power structure. However, by establishing beach-heads in one or more major cities, black revolutionary govern-ments would be in the most strategic position to contend with and eventually defeat this national power structure.

In elaborating its program, the black revolutionary organiza-tion, conscious that the present Constitution was written nearly two centuries ago in an agricultural era when the states had the most rights because they had the most power, also aims to formulate a new Constitution which establishes a new relation-ship of government to people and to property, as well as new relationships between the national government, the states, and the cities, and new relationships between nation-states. Such a Constitution can be the basis for the call to a Constitutional Con-vention and also serve to mobilize national and world support for the black government or governments in the cities where they establish beachheads and where they will have to defend them-selves against the counter-revolutionary forces of the national power structure.

2. They are concentrating on the development of paramilitary cadres ready to defend black militants and the black community from counter-revolutionary attacks. The power which these cadres develop for defense of the community can in turn bring financial support from the community as well as sanctuary, when needed, in the community.

3. The most difficult and challenging task is the organizing of struggles around the concrete grievances of the masses which will not only improve the welfare of the black community but also educate the masses out of their democratic illusions and make them conscious that every administrative and law-enforcing agency in this country is a white power. It is white power which decides whether to shoot to kill (as in Watts) or not to shoot at all (as in Oxford, Mississippi, against white mobs); to arrest or not to arrest; to break up picket lines or not break up picket lines; to investigate brutality and murder or to allow these to go uninvestigated; to decide who eats and who goes on city aid when out of work and who does not eat and does not go on city aid; to decide who goes to what schools and who does not go; who has transportation and who doesn't; who has garbage collected and who doesn't; what streets are lighted and have good sidewalks and what streets have neither lights nor sidewalks; what neighborhoods are torn down for urban renewal and who and what are to go back into these neighborhoods. It is white power which decides which people are drafted into the army to fight and which countries this army is to fight at what moment. It is white power which has brought the United States to the point where it is counter-revolutionary to, and increasingly despised by, the majority of the world's peoples. All these powers are in the political arena, which is the key arena that the black revolutionary movement must take over if there is to be serious black power.

It is extremely important that concrete struggles and marches, picket lines and demonstrations, be focused on the seats of power so that when spontaneous eruptions take place the masses will naturally form committees to take over these institutions rather than concentrate their energies on the places where consumer goods are distributed. Political campaigns to elect black militants to office play a useful role in educating the masses to the importance of political power and the role of government in today's world. They are also a means of creating area organizations. But it should be absolutely clear that no revolution was ever won through the parliamentary process and that as the threat to white power grows, even through the parliamentary process, it will resort to all the naked force at its disposal. At that point, the revolution becomes a total conflict of force against force.

4. The most immediate as well as profound issue affecting the whole black community and particularly black youth is the war in Vietnam. The black revolutionary organization will make it clear in theory and practice that the Vietcong and the Black Power movement in the United States are part of the same worldwide social revolution against the same enemy and that, as this enemy is being defeated abroad, its self-confidence and initiative to act and react are breaking down at home. This is the revolutionary task which Malcolm was undertaking and the reason why he was assassinated. Like the black youth of Watts, the black revolutionary organization will make it clear that black youth have no business fighting in the Ku Klux Klan army that is slaughtering black people in Vietnam. Their job is to defend and better their lives and the lives of their women and children right here. Moreover, speaking from a power base in the big cities even before there is a national revolutionary government, black city governments are the only ones which could seriously talk with the governments of the new nations without resorting to the power that comes out of the barrel of a gun, as the United States must do today.

One final word, particularly addressed to those Afro-Americans who have been brainwashed into accepting white America's characterization of the struggle for black political power as racist. The three forms of struggle in which modern man has engaged are the struggle between nations, the struggle between classes, and the struggle between races. Of these three struggles, the struggle of the colored races against the white race is the one which includes the progressive aspects of the first two and at the same time penetrates most deeply into the essence of the human race or world mankind. The class struggle for economic gains can be, has been, incorporated within the national struggle. Organized labor is among the strongest supporters of the Vietnam war. The struggle of the colored races cannot be blunted in such ways. It transcends the boundaries between nations because historically the colored peoples all over the world constitute a black underclass which has been exploited by the white nations to the benefit of both rich and poor at home.*

In the struggle of the colored peoples of the world for the power to govern themselves, the meaning of man is at stake. Do people of some races exist to be exploited and manipulated by others? Or are all men equal regardless of race? White power was built on the basis of exploiting the colored races of the world for the benefit of the white races. At the heart of this exploitation was the conviction that people of color were not men but sub-human, not self-governing citizens but "natives." White power not only exploited colored peoples economically; it sought systematically to destroy their culture and their personalities and anything else which would compel white people to face the fact that colored peoples are also men. When Western powers fought each other, they fought as men. But when they fought colored peoples, they killed them as natives and as slaves. That is what Western barbarism is doing in Vietnam today. Now the black revolution and the struggle for black power are emerging when all people are clamoring for manhood. Thereby they are destroying forever the idea on which white power has built itself, that some men (whites) are more equal or more capable of self-government (citizenship) than others (colored).

*1965*

---

* Because Afro-Americans were the first people in this country to pose the perspective of revolutionary power to destroy racism, I have been using the word "black" as a *political* designation to refer not only to Afro-Americans but to people of color who are engaged in revolutionary struggle in the United States and all over the world. It should not be taken to mean the domination of Afro-Americans or the exclusion of other people of color from black revolutionary organizations.

# 6

# Black Power:
# A Scientific Concept
# Whose Time Has Come

Black Power. Black Power. This is what is being written about and talked about in all strata of the population of the United States of America. Not since the spector of Communism first began to haunt Europe over one hundred years ago has an idea put forward by so few people frightened so many in so short a time. Liberals and radicals, Negro civil rights leaders and politicians, reporters and editorial writers—it is amazing to what degree all of them are fascinated and appalled by Black Power.

The fact that these words were first shouted out by the little-known Willie Ricks and then by Stokely Carmichael to a crowd of blacks during a march to Jackson, Mississippi, in the spring of 1966 has heightened the tension surrounding the phrase. For earlier in the year the Student Non-Violent Coordinating Committee (SNCC), which Carmichael heads and of which Ricks is an organizer, had issued a public statement on American foreign policy condemning the war in Vietnam as a racist war and connecting the black movement in this country with the anti-imperialist movement in Asia. In that same period, SNCC had begun to analyze the role white liberals and radicals could play in the movement, aptly characterizing it as one of supporting rather than decision-making. Coming after these statements, the cry of Black Power was seen by most people as deepening the gulf between the pro-integrationists and the nationalists. Whether or not Carmichael had intended this cannot really be determined since the phrase had scarcely left his lips before the press and every so-called spokesman for the movement were making their own interpretations to fit their own prejudices or programs.

When Malcolm X was assassinated in February 1965, every

radical in the country and every group in the movement began to seize on some slogan Malcolm had raised or some speech he had made or some facet of his personality in order to identify themselves with him or to establish support for some plank in their own program. The same process of attempted identification is now taking place with Black Power. The difference, however, is that Black Power is not just a personality or a speech or a slogan, as most radicals, liberals, and Negro leaders would like to regard it. The immediate and instinctive reaction of the average white American and the white extremist or fascist is far sounder than that of the liberal, radical, and civil rights leader. For these average whites reacted to the call for Black Power simply and honestly by reaffirming "white power." Their concern is not civil rights (which are, after all, only the common rights which should be guaranteed to everyone by the state and its laws). They are concerned with power, and they recognize instinctively that once the issue of power is raised it means one set of people who are powerless replacing another set of people who have the power. Just as Marx's concept of workers' power did not mean workers becoming a part of or integrating themselves into capitalist power, so Black Power does not mean black people becoming a part of or integrating themselves into white power. Power is not something that a state or those in power bestow upon or guarantee those who have been without power because of morality or a change of heart. It is something that you must make or take from those in power.

It is significant that practically nobody in the United States has tried to seek out the extensive theoretical work that has been done on the concept of Black Power. Actually, most of those writing for and against Black Power don't want to investigate further. They would rather keep the concept vague than grapple with the systematic analysis of American capitalism out of which the concept of Black Power has developed. In *The American Revolution: Pages from a Negro Worker's Notebook*, I stated my belief that if Marx were living today he would have no problem facing the contradictions which have developed since his original analysis because his method of analysis was itself historical. I said further that I considered it the responsibility of any serious

Marxist to advance Marx's theory to meet today's historical situation, in which the underdeveloped—i.e., the super-exploited—nations of the world, which are in fact a world under-class, confront the highly developed capitalist countries in which the working classes for the most part have been incorporated or integrated into pillars of support for the capitalist system. Yet such an analysis has not been seriously attempted by either European or American Marxists. European Marxists have not seriously grappled with: (1) the fact that Marx specifically chose England (at the time the most advanced country industrially in the world) as the basis of his analysis of the class struggle in terms of the process of production; and (2) the fact that at the same time that the European workers were beginning to struggle as a class against the capitalist enemy at home, this same class enemy was expanding its colonial exploitation of Africa, Asia, and Latin America and thereby acquiring the means with which to make concessions to and integrate the working class into the system at home. Therefore, the working classes in the advanced countries were to a significant degree achieving their class progress at home at the expense of the under-class of the world. It was Lenin who dealt with this question most seriously when the European workers supported their capitalist governments in the first imperialist world war, and it was Lenin who, finding it necessary to deal seriously with the anti-colonialist revolutionary struggle after the Russian Revolution, recognized the nationalist and anti-colonialist character of the black struggle in the United States. Yet today, nearly a half century after the Russian Revolution and after two generations of European workers have shown themselves just as opposed to independence for the peoples of Africa and Asia as their capitalist oppressors, European Marxists are still using the slogan "workers of the world, unite" and evading the scientific question of which workers they are calling on.

Who is to unite? And with whom? The under-class of Africa, Asia, and Latin America which makes up the colonized, excolonized, and semi-colonized nations? Or the workers of highly developed Europe and America whose improved conditions and higher standard of living have been made possible by colonial exploitation of the world under-class? Isn't it obvious that the working classes of Europe and America are like the petty bourgeoisie of Marx's time and that they collaborate with the power structure and support the system because their high standard of living depends upon the continuation of this power structure and this system?

The United States has been no exception to this process of advanced nations advancing through exploitation of an under-class excluded from the nation. The only difference has been that its under-class was inside the country, not outside. Black men were brought into this country by a people dedicated to the concept that all blacks were inferior, subhuman savages and natives to be used as tools in the same way that machines are used today. The phrase "all men" defined in the Constitution as "created equal" did not include black men. By definition, blacks were not men but some kind of colored beings. It took 335 years, from 1619 to 1954, before an effort was made to extend the definition of manhood to blacks. Yet American radicals have sought to propagate the concept of "black and white, unite and fight" as if black and white had common issues and grievances, systematically evading the fact that every immigrant who walked off the gangplank into this country did so on the backs of the indigenous blacks and had the opportunity to advance precisely because the indigenous blacks were being systematically deprived of the opportunity to advance by both capitalists and workers.

The United States has a history of racism longer than that of any other nation on earth. Fascism, or the naked oppression of a minority race not only by the state but by the ordinary citizens of the master majority race, is the normal, natural way of life in this country. The confusion and bewilderment of old radicals in the face of the Black Power concept is therefore quite natural. United States and European radicals accept white power as so natural that they do not even see its color. They find it perfectly natural to exhort blacks to integrate into white society and the white structure but cannot conceive of its being the other way around. Integration has been an umbrella under which American radicals have been able to preach class collaboration without appearing to do so. Under the guise of combating the racism of whites, they have actually been trying to bring about collaboration between the oppressed race and the oppressing race, thus sabotaging the revolutionary struggle against oppression which, by virtue of the historical development of the United States, requires a mobilization of the oppressed blacks for struggle against the oppressing whites.

There is no historical basis for the promise, constantly made to blacks by American radicals, that the white workers will join with them against the capitalist enemy. After the Civil War the white workers went homesteading the West while the Southern planters were being given a free hand by Northern capitalists to re-enslave the blacks systematically. White workers supported this re-enslavement just as the German working class supported Hitler in his systematic slaughter of the Jews. The gulf between blacks and white workers in the United States is just as great as that between the Jews and the German workers under Hitler. The difference is that Hitler lasted only a few years while systematic oppression and unceasing threat of death at the hands of ordinary whites have been the lot of blacks in the United States for nearly 400 years. The present so-called white backlash is just white people acting like white people and just as naturally blaming their white hate and white anger not on themselves but on the blacks wanting too much too soon.

Despite their slavish allegiance to the concept of "black and white, unite and fight," most radicals and liberals are well aware that they do not constitute a serious social force in the United States. Few, if any of them, would dare go into a white working-class neighborhood and advocate that slogan. They would be about as safe doing it there as they would be in South Africa. That they go so easily into the black community with the slogan but steer clear of white communities is just another example of how naturally they think white. For whether they admit it to themselves or not, if anyone wanted to build a quick mass organization in a white working-class neighborhood today, his best bet would be to go in as a Ku Klux Klan or White Citizens' Council organizer to mobilize white workers to unite and fight against blacks. Out of self-mobilization white workers have already come up with the slogan: "Fight for what is white and right!"

Revolutionaries must face the fact that the black revolt is now under way and is not waiting for that "someday" when the white workers will have changed their minds about blacks. Like it or not, they must face the fact that the historical and dialectical development of the United States in particular has made the blacks the chief social force for the revolt against American capitalism and that the course of this black revolt itself will decide which side the white workers will be on. The more powerful the black revolt, the more blacks move toward black power, the greater the chances of the white workers' accepting revolutionary change. On the other hand, the more the black revolt is weakened, diluted, and deluded by class collaboration (e.g., "black and white, unite and fight" and "integration"), the more chance there is of the white workers remaining counter-revolutionary.

Black Power in the United States raises the same question that Stalin could not tolerate from Mao: Would the revolution in China come from the urban workers or from the peasantry? Mao pursued his theory, based upon the specific conditions in China, and was proven right by the revolution itself. In the United States today, the question is whether the blacks (over 75 percent of whom are now concentrated in the heart of the nation's largest cities) will lead the revolution or whether they must wait for the white workers. In the twentieth century the United States has advanced rapidly from a semi-urban, semi-rural society into an overwhelmingly urban society. The farms which at the beginning of the century still employed nearly half the working population have now become so mechanized that the great majority of those who formerly worked on the land have had to move into the cities. Their land is now the city streets. Meanwhile, industry itself has been automated, with the result that black labor, which over the centuries has been systematically deprived of the opportunity to become skilled, has become economically and socially unnecessary. Unemployed or underemployed, the now expendable blacks are a constant threat to the system. Not only must they be fed in order to cool off the chances of their rebelling, but they occupy the choicest and most socially critical land in the heart of the nation's cities from which the racist white population has fled in order to remain lily white. Moreover, since blacks have become a majority in the inner-city population, they are now in line to assume the political leadership of the cities in accordance with the historical tradition whereby the largest ethnic minorities have successively run the cities. The city is now the black man's land, and the city is also the place where the nation's most critical problems are concentrated.

Confronted with this dilemma, the power structure, from its highest echelons to the middle classes, is seeking to incorporate or integrate a few elite Negroes into the system and thereby behead the black movement of its leadership. At the same time the power structure has devised ingenious methods for mass "Negro removal." Under the pretext of "urban renewal," it condemns and breaks up entire black communities, bulldozes homes, and scatters the black residents to other black communities which in turn are judged to need "urban renewal." Meanwhile, under the auspices of white draft boards black youths are sent as cannon fodder to die in the counter-revolutionary wars which the United States is carrying on all over the world as it replaces the old European colonial powers. Today the sun never sets on an American Empire which maintains bases in at least fifty-five different worldwide locations. The war in Vietnam is a war of sections of the world under-class fighting one another, for it is the poor, uneducated, unemployed who are drafted and the privileged (mainly white) who are deferred. This United States counter-revolution all over the world has the support not only of the general population but of organized labor. A peace demonstration in any white working-class or middle-class neighborhood brings out a hostile mob which is sure to come even when the peace demonstrators are allegedly guarded by police.

Those progressives who are honestly confused by the concept of Black Power are in this state of confusion because they have not scientifically evaluated the present stage of historical development in relation to the stage of historical development when Marx projected the concept of workers' power vs. capitalist power. Yesterday the concept of workers' power expressed the revolutionary social force of the working class organized inside the process of capitalist production. Today the concept of Black

Power expresses the new revolutionary social force of the black population concentrated in the black belt of the South and in the urban ghettos of the North—a revolutionary social force which must struggle not only against the capitalists but against the workers and middle classes who benefit by and support the system which has oppressed and exploited blacks. To expect the Black Power struggle to embrace white workers inside the black struggle is in fact to expect the revolution to welcome the enemy into its camp. To speak of the common responsibility of all Americans, white and black, to fight for black liberation is to sponsor class collaboration.

The uniqueness of Black Power stems from the specific historical development of the United States. It has nothing to do with any special moral virtue in being black, as some black nationalists seem to think. Nor does it have to do with the special cultural virtues of the African heritage. Identification with the African past is useful insofar as it enables black Americans to develop a sense of identity independent of the Western civilization which has robbed them of their humanity by robbing them of any history. But no past culture ever created a revolution. Every revolution creates a new culture out of the process of revolutionary struggle against the old values and culture which an oppressing society has sought to impose upon the oppressed.

The chief virtue in being black at this juncture in history stems from the fact that the vast majority of the people in the world who have been deprived of the right of self-government and self-determination are people of color. Today these people of color are not only the wretched of the earth but people in revolutionary ferment, having arrived at the decisive recognition that their undevelopment is not the result of ethnic backwardness but of their systematic confinement to backwardness by the colonial powers. The struggle against this systematic deprivation is what has transformed them into a social force or an under-class.

The clarion call "black people of the world, unite and fight" is only serious if it is also a call to black people to organize. The call for Black Power in the United States at this juncture in the development of the movement has gone beyond the struggle for civil rights to a call for black people to replace white people in power. Black people must organize the fight for power. They have nothing to lose but their condition as the wretched of the earth.

The call for Black Power is creating—had to create—splits within the movement. These splits are of two main kinds. The first is between the Black Power advocates and the civil rights advocates. The civil rights advocates, sponsored, supported, and dependent upon the white power structure, are committed to integrate blacks into the white structure without any serious changes in that structure. In essence, they are simply asking to be given the same rights which whites have had and blacks have been denied. By equality they mean just that and no more: being equal to white Americans.

This is based on the assumption that the American way of life (and American democracy) is itself a human way of life, an ideal worth striving for. Specifically and concretely and to a large extent consciously, the civil rights advocates evade the fact that the American way of life is a way of life that has been achieved through systematic exploitation of others (chiefly the black people inside this country and the Latin Americans, and is now being maintained and defended by counter-revolutionary force against blacks everywhere, particularly in Asia and Africa.

Inside the Black Power movement there is another growing split between the idealists or romanticists and the realists. The romanticists continue to talk and hope to arouse the masses of black people through self-agitation, deluding themselves and creating the illusion that one set of people can replace another set of people in power without building an organization to take active steps toward power, while at the same time agitating and mobilizing the masses. Masses and mass support come only when masses of people not only glimpse the desirability and possibility of serious improvement in their condition, but can see the force and power able to bring this about.

The realists in the movement for Black Power base themselves first and foremost on a scientific evaluation of the American system and of revolution, knowing that Black Power cannot come from the masses doing what they do when they feel like doing it, but must come from the painstaking, systematic building of an organization to lead the masses to power. The differentiation now taking place inside the Black Power movement between idealists and realists is comparable to the classic differentiation which took place inside the Russian revolutionary movement between the Mensheviks, who were opposed to building disciplined organization, and the Bolsheviks, who insisted upon it.

The organization for Black Power must concentrate on the issue of political power and refuse to redefine and explain away Black Power as "black everything except black political power." The development of technology in the United States has made it impossible for blacks to achieve economic power by the old means of capitalist development. The ability of capitalists today to produce in abundance not only makes competition with them on an economic capitalist basis absurd but has already brought the United States technologically to the threshold of a society where each can have according to his needs. Thus black political power, coming at this juncture in the economically advanced United States, is the key not only to black liberation but to the introduction of a new society to emancipate economically the masses of the people in general. For black political power will have to decide on the kind of economy and the aims and direction of the economy for the people.

"The City Is the Black Man's Land" (pp. 39-50) laid the basis for the development of the type of organization which would be in tune with the struggle for Black Power. Such an organization must be clearly distinguished not only from the traditional civil rights organizations which have been organized and financed by whites to integrate blacks into the system, and thereby save it, but also from the *ad hoc* organizations which have sprung up in the course of the struggle, arousing the masses emotionally around a particular issue and relying primarily on the enthusiasm and good will of their members and supporters for their continuing activity. By contrast, an organization for Black Power must be a cadre-type organization whose members have a clear understanding, allegiance, and dedication to the organization's perspectives and objectives and who have no illusions about the necessities of a struggle for power.

A cadre organization cannot be made up of just enthusiastic and aroused people. Its essential core must be cold, sober individuals who are ready to accept discipline and who recognize the absolute necessity of a strong leadership which can organize and project a strategy of action to mobilize the conscious and-not-so-conscious masses around their issues and grievances for a life-and-death struggle against those in power. Such a cadre must be able to continue the revolutionary struggle despite the inevitable setbacks because they believe that only through the revolution will their own future be assured.

At the same time that it recognizes the inevitability of setbacks, such an organization must build itself consciously upon a perspective of victory. This is particularly necessary in the United States, where the idea of the defeat of the black man has been so systematically instilled into the black people themselves that a tendency toward self-destruction or martyrdom will lurk unconsciously within the organization unless it is systematically rooted out of every member, leader, and supporter. The movement for Black Power cannot afford to lose other Malcolms, other Emmett Tills, other Medgar Everses, and it must build the kind of organization which has the strength and discipline to assure that there will be no more of these.

Nor can such an organization build itself on the counter-revolution's mistakes or abuses of the masses as the civil rights movement has done. Rather it must seriously plot every step of its course—when to act, when to retreat, when to seize upon an issue or a mistake by the ruling power and when not to.

Within such a cadre there must be units able to match every type of unit that the counter-revolution has at its disposal, able not only to pit themselves against these but to defend them. Colonialism, whether in Asia, Africa, Latin America, or inside the United States, was established by the gun and is maintained by the gun. But it has also been able to hold itself together because it had skilled, disciplined colonizers and administrators well versed in the art of ruling and able to make the decisions inseparable from rule.

There will be many fundamental questions and problems facing such an organization as it moves toward power. How will it create new national and international ties with other people within the country and without? What will it do about industry when its take-over is imminent and those in power resist? What will it do about the armed forces and how will it win them over? In what cities or localities should a base first be built? What will it do when confronted by those in power as they respond to the threat of replacement? What segments of the old apparatus can be useful and which should be destroyed? And most important, how can it expose its alleged friends as the real enemies they are? These are all questions of strategy and tactics which every serious organization for power has to work out but which no serious organization for power would write too much about.

As I said in *The American Revolution,* the tragedy is that so few see the urgency of facing up to this reality. But as I also said, that is what makes a revolution: two sides—the revolution and the counter-revolution—and the people on both sides.

*1966*

# 7
# Culture
# and
# Black Power

Recently I attended a conference on Black Culture. As I sat there looking at all the beautiful black faces, I could see in them the drive, the desire, the compassion, and also the hope that in that meeting and out of that meeting they could find the unity to take them down Freedom Road. And yet inside myself I could feel only a seething. A seething because there were so many things that I wanted to say, things I wanted to tell my people, things that I thought they should know and would understand if only I could put them in a form that would show them where they had come from and where they were going. I wanted to stand up before them and say, "Look at me, look at my face. Am I not black just like you? Look at the lines in my face. Could I not have been Emmett Till's uncle standing in that doorway in Mississippi when the two white men came? Can't you just hear me saying, 'Don't take the boy, boss; please don't take the boy. He's just a little old boy from Chicago. He don't know no better. Boss, don't take the boy; don't hurt the boy.' Yes, I could have been Emmett Till's uncle. And the little girls in Birmingham. Couldn't I have been a cousin or a brother to one of them? Can't you just see my standing there sobbing over their little bodies which have been bombed into oblivion? Or couldn't I have been a relative of that African rebel who, long long years ago, dived into the sea rather than allow himself to be brought in chains to this continent? Could I not have been any one of these? Look at my face. What do you see in it?"

But that wasn't all that I wanted to say. I wanted to say to them, "You speak of all the miracles and the grandeur and the splendor of our ancestors in the yesteryears of Africa. But don't you know that we are living today in an age of new miracles? Two years from now a man will be walking on the moon, and what only a few years ago was to most people mainly a beautiful symbol of love and of the unknown will be a walking place for men. And the first men to land on the moon and set up a colony there will be initiating a phenomenon that will dominate world history for the next 500 years—that is, if by that time we have not all been blown out of world history by that power man has today because Marco Polo brought gunpowder back from China several hundred years ago.

"All that knowledge is in me too. Can't you see it in my face? And all of it is in you as well. And we have to remember that today we are in a different age and that now when we think of our culture, we have to think not only of where we were at one time in history, but where we are today and where we are going. For what good is all that culture if we cannot use it as a stepping stone to take us into the last quarter of the twentieth century?"

And as they talked of African kings and princes and the deeds and miracles that these performed and of which they are so proud, I wanted to tell them, "Yes, all of that is us. But the miracles of today are ours as well. When Thomas Edison created a light bulb, he created a miracle greater than those of Jesus of Nazareth because he gave us light by which to walk the streets at night. For at the time of Jesus of Nazareth, it was often impossible to walk the roads because of the thugs who waylaid men along the way." I wanted to tell them that when our mothers were giving birth to us, this light made it possible for the doctors to perform the miracles that enabled mothers and babies to survive, just as it has been the invention of the freezer which has made it possible to keep medicine in the sterile form needed by these doctors. And I wanted to tell them, "If you don't believe me, just ask some of our young black chemists. We have many of them now who will verify what I have told you, and they are just as much a part of our future as you are. And like me, they know that the foods we eat and which you are particular not to eat are no longer harmful. They know, as I do, that in every age, in every country, men have eaten particular types of food because these were suited to the climate and to the surroundings of the particular country. If they lived near the sea, they ate fish; if they lived inland, they ate other foods, particularly grains from agriculture. But today if any food (no matter where it might have been grown) is clean and refrigerated so that it won't spoil, it is not harmful. These are some of the miracles that modern man has brought about in the age of industrialization, miracles which are ours whether black men invented them or not."

But more than that, I wanted to tell them that we are already living in an age of power and that the power of America, which is reflected every time and everywhere it breathes in the world, comes from the fact that it has brought together the cultures and peoples of so many continents. I wanted to tell them that the African culture of which they spoke so proudly and lovingly should chiefly be the basis for our feeling the need to wrest some of this power from these American giants so that they will not be able to control what happens to the Africa from whence we came. And when some said that they wanted to go back to that Africa, I wanted to scream at them, "How do you expect to go back? In the first place, who will let you get on the plane or the boat? Might not the Man say that you can't go, that you are only going back to start trouble? And even if you were lucky enough to get away on the boat or plane, isn't it possible that a torpedo or missile could hit it just a few miles away from the African shores (to be reported afterwards as as just a terrible shipwreck or disintegration of the plane in the air)? All that is power. And even if you then escaped from the sinking boat or the crashed plane, might not some black African be standing there as you arrive, ready to bash out your brains with the barrel of a gun because the white bwana had told him these Negroes had only come to start trouble? This is what is happening in Africa today. And what country in Africa could you go to and be away from the Man, who has prolonged your agony for so many centuries in the United States? What country could you go to, if you please? What country is there in Africa which has no neo-colonial boss telling the Africans what they can do, when they can do it, and how they have to do it?

"We can't escape our destiny. Our destiny is right in this country. It is here in this country because it has been on our backs that all the immigrants who have come to this continent and helped it grow and of whom Americans speak so proudly have walked as they came off the gangplank. It has been on our backs that they walked off. Out of *our* blood, sweat, and toil have come the riches that have made America great, and it is we whose struggle can change America from a land in which men walk up the ladder on the backs of others into a land where each man walks in the sun equal to everyone else."

And there was still more that I wanted to tell them. I wanted to tell them that the question of why we are as we are is nothing that was decided on a majority/minority basis. In every country, including even our beloved Africa, it has always been a minority which ruled. And this minority has ruled because it has had power. Take the United States, for example. If the twenty largest industrialists who control the industrial heart of this country were to decide tomorrow that they want every black man to be able to walk the streets as free as he pleased, not one white person in this country would dare to say no (provided that each of them knew in advance that if they said no they would lose their jobs). It's not the President who has this power, mind you, and he was presumably elected by the majority, but just these twenty largest industrialists who are a very small minority and who were never elected by any majority, but who still have this power to throw people out of work. This is what I wanted to tell them. I wanted to remind them that it is the minority which rules. All they have to do is look at South Africa, where a small minority can tell the African majority where they can walk, where they can't walk, where they can sleep, and where they can work. And the same is true in practically every country. A minority rules because it has the power to rule. That is what I mean when I say that blacks must have power.

Take, for example, the police. When I talk about the police, I don't mean getting a few more blacks on the police force to make it look like the police force is hiring blacks in proportion to their numbers. No, what I am talking about is the power to be police commissioner, so that when I lay down the rules it makes no difference who is on that force, black or white. They obey the rules I lay down or they lose their jobs. The police commissioner in every city in the United States right now—in Chicago, New York, Cleveland—could fire every white on the force and hire blacks to take their places. And in the morning he could tell those blacks to go out on the streets and whip some black folks, and they would do it because he had this power to tell them what to do. Likewise, a black police commissioner could lay off every black policeman on the force and bring in whites in their places, and they would have to follow his orders. That is what I am talking about when I speak about power.

It is the same with education. He who controls the board of education, the superintendent of schools, and the finances of education is the one who decides what kind of education our children get. It doesn't mean that all the whites have to be taken out. But it does mean blacks having the power to tell the principals and teachers, no matter what their color, what they should teach and how they should teach it—because it is black children who are suffering most under the present system of education. And that is what we mean when we say that it is necessary to move into the arena of power and take power by whatever means necessary.

People talk about housing. Is it a question of a few more black people getting into some housing projects or into some homes in the outer city from which whites are fleeing? Or does it mean blacks at the head of the housing commission deciding what kind of housing, when it is going to be built, and where it is going to be built because it is the black people who are the ones in most desperate need of decent housing? This doesn't mean that architects, contractors, plumbers, brick masons of all colors won't be needed to build these houses. But it does mean who will have the power to decide what kind of housing, when, where, and how.

Seek ye first the political kingdom and all things will be added unto you.

That role is not easy. But we know, and need to admit to ourselves for once, that a lot of our ancestors came here because some tribal chiefs who were just as black in hue as they were went out and kidnapped them and sold them into bondage for a rifle or a barrel of rum. These African chiefs had the *power* of life and death over other Africans. We also know that immigrants

who were supposed to have come in freedom from other countries practically came in bondage because in the countries from
which they came, some people had the power to say that they
must leave the country or lose their lives.

Oh, there were so many things I wanted to tell them so that
they would have a vision of the possibilities of the future. I
wanted to remind them that we are not going back to the farm
or each to his garden, that the farms have been outmoded and
that in a few short years the Kingdom of the Sea may produce
far more of the food the world needs than even the richest farmlands of this country, that there will be ships and fleets of ships
bringing countless riches in minerals and foods back from the
bottom of the sea, and at the same time people in laboratories
will be producing more food in a few days than all the people
now working on the land. That is the kind of future we must be
preparing for.

I wanted to tell them about the future that lies ahead of us in
education, where instead of blackboards we will have TV screens,
where by a turn of the switch we can bring to people the accumulated wealth of science, literature, history, mathematics.
And not only will grading be done by computers, but even the
classrooms will be swept clean by centrally controlled machines.

This is the age of miracles in which our children's minds are
growing up. It is an age where in cold climates all the houses can
be heated by the sun and in the hot climate the houses can be
cooled by air-conditioning. It is an age where we will soon be
able to turn on our faucets and draw from them milk and other
beverages piped into our homes as water is today. I wanted to
remind them, too, that many of them had come to that conference in jet planes which had whisked them in two or four hours
further than Columbus could travel in as many weeks.

Of what profit, then, is our history and our culture unless it is
used in a vision of our future? For if our ancestors were kings
and sat on golden thrones, of what avail were those thrones
against the gunpowder which Marco Polo had introduced to
Western civilization? It was this same gunpowder which gave
Europe the power to go into Africa and wrest it away from our
ancestors. Had they not Balkanized our Africa, would kings still

be sitting on their thrones, or would Africa today be one of the most developed continents in the world? Who knows, and who can say that it would not have been? But for us who have lived in twentieth-century society, there is one thing we should be sure of, and that is that the road is not back, but ahead to power.

Some of you laugh and scoff when you read in the American press that Mao Tse-tung says that power comes out of the barrel of a gun. But nobody in the world should know that better than he. Because he knows that all the culture in China could not stand up against Western civilization once that civilization had mastered the gunpowder it took from China. He knows this because this power was used against him. And because the United States has this gunpowder, it has bases all around the world, in Asia, in Africa, in South America; and it is able to keep these bases not because Asians and Africans and Latins are inferior, but because the United States has so much power—power not only to control the markets and the commodity prices of the world, but firepower to destroy anyone who threatens this control.

The Chinese have a great deal of culture, as all the world knows. But Mao Tse-tung, cultured as he was, did not sit around and talk about the virtues of being yellow and boast about his yellow ancestors. No. He said, "Because we have been, so we shall be." And today the Chinese are spending their time trying to build the most powerful country in the world and developing their lands and minerals and training their people in mind and body so that they can step forward into the twentieth and twenty-first centuries with power. Gird up your armor. Face up to reality. For whether we get beat up in the alley by a cop, whether our kids go without an education and end up in Vietnam, whether they work or eat, whether they sleep in a decent house or in a rat-infested shack, whether they are tossed into a river with irons around their necks or whether they sit in the halls of Congress or in the White House or in a general's seat at military headquarters is a question of power. And we shall have power, or we shall perish in the streets.

*1966*

# 8

# The Basic Issues
# and the
# State of the Nation

It is fitting that I should be the keynote speaker at this consultation, not because I'm a great speaker but because up to now white people from all strata of life and organization have been investigating and studying black folks. Never have they felt that black folks were intellectually capable of studying white folks and deciding what should be done about this society which white folks call the greatest society on earth—without realizing that it is great for white folks only because it has been a living hell for black folks.

If at this juncture I have any concrete proposal to make to seriously concerned white folks as to what they can or should do, I would propose that they support a black foundation to make a revolutionary study of how black folks can take power from white folks and the kind of society that must be built when black folks take power.

The American people have evaded the issues that I am going to pose today for so long that the question of whether or not they will be able to resolve them is the furthest from my mind.

Back in the early 1960's, at the time of the burning of the buses in Anniston, Alabama, which is not far from Birmingham, I proposed to the UAW that it immediately dispatch a busload of workers, black and white, to Alabama to test what the Klan in 'Bama would do. I was, of course, not only interested in testing the Alabama Klan. I was also testing the readiness of the organized labor movement and of Northern white workers to clash with other whites on the issue of integration—which they allegedly supported, particularly because all the action was taking place down South.

The UAW took the easy way out. Instead of confronting the rank and file with this proposal, the leadership made a financial contribution to the NAACP—an organization which had already discredited itself by ousting Robert Williams from the presidency of its Monroe, North Carolina, branch because he had advocated black people defending themselves from nightriding terrorist Klansmen (in his famous "meet violence with violence" proposal). Today, nearly seven years later, the same Northern white workers who thought it was so noble for black men and women not to defend themselves and their children from howling, club-swinging mobs in the South have formed part of cursing, howling, bottle-throwing mobs in the North and are openly arming and calling upon official and unofficial bodies to equip themselves with the most modern weaponry to try to push blacks back into their places.

It was this same bus-burning incident which caused me, at that time chairman of a small radical newspaper called *Correspondence,* to write an article entitled, "The Second Civil War Has Begun in the U.S.A." There was much heated debate in the organization (which was primarily white) over this article. People argued that a civil war situation did not exist in the United States on the race issue because there were not enough people on each side clashing over fundamental issues. After all, they said, blacks were only asking to be like whites and to be a part of the system. They weren't clashing with whites and they weren't clashing with the system.

In one sense their argument was a sound one. At that time, black people were still appealing to the moral conscience of America. They were only asking for the civil rights which are, after all, only the normal rights which a nation grants to its citizens. Black people had not yet learned that rights are what you make and take, and that it takes power to beget rights and even more power to secure and ensure those rights after they have been begotten. Black people had also not yet realized that any claims which the American people—Christian, atheist, or agnostic—had to moral behavior had been refuted by their own history. This nation was built on the extermination of one race and the systematic degradation of another. First it saw nothing wrong in fighting a war to free itself from a colonial oppression and then continuing to keep blacks in colonial oppression. Nearly a hundred years later it again saw nothing wrong in allegedly fighting a civil war to free those blacks from slavery and then making a compromise with those it had fought to establish a new form of servitude for these blacks, so that the nation could go on its merry way industrializing itself with the labor of immigrants. But this history you all know.

What is new is that we are now in the early stages of another civil war and the system which was created by the last civil war is collapsing all around us. *The key to the future lies in being able to resist the temptation to reform the system so that it can work.* It is not difficult to recognize that a system is in trouble. What is difficult is to recognize this and at the same time recognize that *all* attempts to reform the system will in the end only create more bitterness and conflict with those forces already in motion, forces which can only survive by transforming the system from top to bottom. The example of Vietnam should always be kept in mind. In Vietnam, anything short of total revolutionary control of the entire country by the National Liberation Front—in other words, any attempt to set up other institutions to reform the system as the United States is attempting to do with one South Vietnam government after another—means a bloody and extended civil war. *The only way to make the civil war briefer and less bloody is to hasten the destruction of the system by the revolutionary social forces.*

So I am not here today to tell you how to save the system. Rather I am here to help you hasten its demise and to prepare yourselves for a new leadership and a new system.

Now why did I say back in 1961 that the second civil war had begun in the United States—even though at that time I was not quite as sure of my ground as I am today? And what is the difference between the issues that were posed in the first civil war and those that are posed in today's civil war?

The first civil war was fought because one force in American society—the industrialists and the working people in the North—wanted to be the ones to decide how the West should be developed, while another force, in the South, had its own plans for developing the West. The issue was whether the West should be developed as a wheat-growing country by homesteading Northerners to act as a breadbasket for the rapidly industrializing North, or whether it should be cotton country developed by slave-owning Southerners. In other words, the issue was who should control or who should have power in the West. The issue was *not* any general principle of slave labor vs. free labor and certainly not the specific issue of slave labor vs. free labor in the South.

Once you understand this, you can understand why it was so easy for the North to make the infamous Compromise of 1877 which allowed the South to re-introduce a new form of servitude for its black people. The American people always prefer to think that they are fighting for great moral principles rather than admit that the real issue is one of power and control. This genius for disguising real issues of power as moral issues of principle is one of the chief reasons why we are today faced with a second civil war. And this second civil war is potentially much more complex and dangerous for two reasons:

1. Because it is going to be fought between two sets of people of two different races. One set of one race has been systematically damned into underdevelopment in every facet of its daily life, political, economic, and social, by another set of another race which has at the same time pretended that both races were equal, but which has discriminated against blacks on the basis of race and thus created in black people a sense of their identity as a race and as a people. The first set, the oppressed race, can therefore only free itself from the second set, the oppressing race, by liberating itself as a race. Thus it is for blacks a war of national liberation, to free themselves as black people from white America, past, present, and future, from its culture, its way of thinking, its history, its economic system and its politics.

2. The conflict is not only national but international. Because the same set of white people who have colonized black people at home have done and are continuing to do the same thing to people of color all over the world.

How have we arrived at this point?

1. For years radicals and liberals have been calling for unity

between white workers and black workers on the theory that white and black were only divided by an external force, the ruling class, which is supposed to have created the division so that it could rule. But what this theoretical construct of "divide and rule" has failed to recognize is that the so-called lack of unity between white and black is and has been in reality an antagonism between white workers and black people, the kind of antagonism which is inevitable between oppressor and oppressed.

2. When blacks were unable to get their rights through moral appeal, they began to realize that they had to get them through power.

3. Getting something through power means one set of people who are powerless replacing another set of people who are in power.

4. Power is always concrete. It involves control of very concrete resources and institutions: (a) *Economic resources and institutions,* such as banks and industries and stores; (b) *political resources and institutions,* such as local, state, and national governments, courts, and police forces; (c) *social resources and institutions,* such as schools and universities, churches, public places, foundations, etc.

Step by step, as black people have rid themselves of the old rag thoughts of moral misconceptions which cluttered up their minds, and as white people have revealed their determination to hold onto the resources and institutions of power, the clash has become inevitable.

As usual, the more that those in power are determined to hold onto their power, the more phrases they use to disguise the real issue. So today, everywhere, the hue and cry is that we must save democracy, enforce law and order, protect majority rule, defend property rights, save the free world, restore liberty and equality, etc., etc.—all the empty phrases of those who know that their power is being challenged and who are determined not to yield any real power.

To have some vision of what is necessary we must start not at the bottom but at the very top of this collapsing society. It is a cold fact that neither the present President of the United States nor any of his aides nor any of the present aspirers to the presidency of the United States could possibly resolve either the chief international issue or the chief domestic issue which faces this nation. The reason is that none of them from the moment that they began to exercise any power could gain or maintain the confidence of the Third World either inside or outside this nation. There is no reason for any of the black nations of the world—which constitute the majority of the world's people—to believe that the United States, as long as it is ruled by whites, could make a binding treaty that would respect their national sovereignty. The American people say that they believe in majority rule. Yet less than 200 million Americans are led to believe that they, a minority in the world, are entitled to use all necessary force and all the force at their disposal to decide the course of the world. This is something that no nation in the world's history has ever been foolish enough to accept as its responsibility or its destiny. Only a black people in power in this country could sign a treaty safeguarding the national sovereignty of other nations and setting up fair trade and technical exchange relations with other nations which could be acknowledged and respected by other nations.

The first civil war was fought over who should control the West. This civil war is to be fought over who should control the cities. In every major city inside this country black people are fast becoming the biggest ethnic majority, driven to the cities by the agricultural revolution in the South where they were at one time the only working class, but where their labor is no longer needed. They are also being driven to the cities for political reasons because, if they remain in the counties of the South, they would soon constitute the ruling power in county government by virtue of majority rule. But when it comes to black people, the beautiful principle of majority rule is no longer a principle, in the North or the South—just as when it came to the slaves in ancient Greece the beautiful principle of democracy was no longer a principle. Throughout the North, as is now obvious, the whites have run away to the suburbs, abandoning the inner cities to the blacks. Yet they still want to run the cities from the suburbs, using their blue occupation army of police to maintain their control of the reservation at night until they return the next morning to civilize it by their presence. That is how Washington, D.C., is controlled, and the rest of the country follows the pattern of the nation's capital.

It is obvious that blacks must rule the city from top to bottom. But it is not simply a question of the city because the cities are part of a nation. So the city must change its relation to the federal and the state governments. New city-federal relations must be developed in place of the city-state relations that have never been adequate to supply the social and economic needs of the city. These in turn require a new federal constitution. Therefore, black political power in the city is not only a challenge to the suburban whites who want to continue to rule the city and who are devising all kinds of multi-county regional schemes to do so; it is also a direct challenge to the federal government. But the federal government, which is constantly being called upon to intervene in local, city, and state matters, is ruling on the basis of a set of constitutional rules and procedures whose establishment black people had nothing to do with, primarily because the white Founding Fathers, the world's original fascists, thought of blacks only as things and not as people.

Thus the question of *whose* constitution, *whose* law and order, *whose* equality, *whose* justice, *whose* welfare, becomes a question of what kind of constitution, what kind of law and order, what kind of equality, what kind of justice, what kind of welfare; and the need arises to create a new constitution, a new law and order, a new equality, a new justice, a new welfare—in other words, a new political, economic, and social system.

Let me say right here that no whites can participate directly in the resolution of any of these issues until or unless they have recognized that other whites—not only those in power, but those who support the ones in power (which means the majority of whites)—are their enemy.

What does recognition of these whites as an enemy mean?

1. It means recognizing that you can't change them by moral persuasion or reason. This is the first old rag thought that seriously concerned whites have to throw out. Only then will you be able to understand that a clash and a struggle for power between

you and them is inevitable and only then will you be able to prepare for such a clash.

2. It means recognizing that those in power and those who support the whites in power are a direct danger and threat not only to the black man but to you. Only then will you recognize that it is a matter of survival, i.e., a matter of life and death, for *you* to take power away from those in power. If you can't recognize this, then you had better join them—or they will have to crush you as well.

Only when some whites begin to act upon these fundamental recognitions and achieve some power by virtue of acting on these foundations can there be a meeting of some whites with power with some blacks in power to work out new constitutional procedures under which they can co-exist.

The chief need is to recognize that we are already in the early stages of a great conflict between the revolution and the counter-revolution, both inside the country and outside the country, a conflict which can end only in the victory of the revolution or in the common ruin of the contending forces.

This conflict already has its own momentum. We here have very little to do with that momentum, nor could we do much to alter it if we wanted to.

But if this conference accepts that all concepts under which we have previously lived have now become old rags which must be torn up and thrown out, then we have the responsibility to begin to work out new concepts. Nor am I saying that we can work them out together, because it is very difficult for the landlord to listen to the tenant, and it is even harder for those who are identified with those in power in every way except in intentions to recognize that the party is over and that it is not whether or not you like it but the cold realities which force the re-evaluation.

You will note that I have not mentioned the church. Whatever it could have done or should have done, it too is caught up in the whirlwind of the revolution. Castro delivered the best message to the church in the early 1960's when America thought it could use the church against the revolution. In his May Day speech in 1961, published in the same issue of *Correspondence* which announced that the second civil war had begun in the United States, Castro made two important points about the Christian church. First, he said Christianity originated as the religion of the humble, the slaves, and the oppressed of Rome. Second, he reminded the church that it had been able to co-exist with the Roman Empire, with feudalism, with the absolute monarchies, and with the democratic republican bourgeoisie, always adapting itself. Why then should it not be able to "co-exist with a regime which in its social laws and social perspectives, in its defense of human interests and its defense of all men in society, in its struggle against exploitation, is so much more like Christianity than are the exploitation and cruelty of feudalism, the absolute monarchs, the Roman Empire, the republican bourgeosie or Yankee imperialism?"

Today most churchgoers are part and parcel of "the Man"—no better, no worse. Only history will absolve them, and even history, after blacks get some power, may not be so kind.

*1967*

# 9
# The Future
# Belongs
# to the Dispossessed

# The Future
# Belongs
# to the Dispossessed

With the end of World War II came the beginning of the end of colonialism. Colonialism, with the possible exception of the early settling of North and South America, had been the racial occupation of territories already occupied by people of color, by colorless people who had the express purpose of exploiting the indigenous population. The colorless people were free to go everywhere and dominate, while the people of color were confined to geographical areas to be exploited economically, socially, and politically. At the end of World War I, Marcus Garvey thought the old colonial powers were weak enough to allow him and his fellow blacks to be able to re-capture some of Africa for the descendants of Africa in the Western Hemisphere. The time was not quite ripe. But by the end of World War II, black people in Africa, Asia, and Latin America were ready to struggle to recapture some of their land for themselves. The first two world wars had been wars among the old colonial powers over the dispossessed peoples of Africa, Asia, and Latin America. After World War II all future wars would be wars between the possessing and the dispossessed.

The old European powers, confronted with Russian Communism in Europe, were too weak to defend themselves against the onrushing tide of self-determination by the dispossessed. They did what those who rule always try to do when confronted by rebellion: they tried to appease their subjects by granting them a form of "home rule" called independence, and encouraging them to become carbon copies of the mother country by practicing "democracy." Since democracy is a luxury which can be indulged in only by those strong enough not to be subverted by external powers, these new nations became ripe for neo-colonialism. For what European country had ever practiced democracy before it had built up a power base? Even the United States did not write its Constitution until it had expropriated entire nations of indigenous Indians and had set up a system of imported slave labor to accumulate its economic power.

Today, with most of the African nations torn by domestic intrigue and civil strife, fostered primarily by agents of the colonial powers who are in turn propped up by the United States, the United States has turned its full attention to Asia. It is confident that by intrigue and the armed might of Portugal, South Africa and Rhodesia, Africa can be kept in sufficient turmoil so that it will be unable to rule itself for another decade. Africa has been so balkanized by the imperialisms of the past and the intrigues of the present that it will probably be unable to unite along the lines of the Pan-Africanism laid down by Nkrumah without a continent-wide war of blacks against whites. But Asia is not Africa.

World War I interrupted the full colonialization and balkanization of mainland Asia. The ensuing communist revolution in China provided the momentum for nationalist revolutions free of democratic illusions and therefore able to resist and defend themselves against neo-colonialism. India was the only large nation trapped in democracy, and is today the best example of the failure of democracy in an ex-colonial country. Democracy enables the capitalists and landlords to keep the workers in economic misery and poverty and to use the armed powers of the state to suppress their spontaneous outbursts in bread strikes, hunger strikes, language strikes, etc. Meanwhile, the communist revolution in China has not only achieved success in the form of the overthrow of the American-sponsored Chiang Kai-shek regime, but following the seizure of power it has gone far beyond any other revolution in history, including the Russian Revolution. Through the Cultural Revolution, it has been able to achieve a revolution within a revolution to prevent those in power from becoming entrenched in the no longer revolutionary ideas of the past. Thus it has created a base of support and inspiration for all other potential revolutionary forces in Asia.

Since the old European powers—England, France, and Holland —have been chased out of Asia and are too weak to maintain armies large enough to challenge China's, and since no country on the Asian mainland is powerful enough to contest China, the United States stands isolated, the only power left from the old colonial wolfpack which emerged from World War I with enough might to try to stem the world revolution for independence and self-determination building up in the black nations. The United States calls itself the protector of the "free world," referring to those powers which were free to dominate and exploit black people because black peoples were not strong enough to resist them. The United States is therefore trying to keep the black peoples of the world in a state of continued weakness and dependency. In Europe, the United States did not have to resort to counter-revolutionary war to shore up the North Atlantic nations against Russian Communism. The Marshall Plan was sufficient because Russian Communism's expansion was not revolutionary. In Asia, the United States has resorted to counter-revolutionary war when confronted by revolution. Counter-revolution in a time of world revolution or continental revolution always assumes the form of counter-revolutionary war. That is the form it assumed in the Europe of the French Revolution, when the monarchs of Europe allied themselves to fight against "Liberty, Equality, and Fraternity." That is the form it assumed again in Europe after World War I, when the capitalist nations of the West allied to fight against the successful Bolshevik Revolution in Russia. Today the counter-revolution is directed against the people in all those countries which, having been systematically damned into underdevelopment, are seeking to chart their own course toward development. These people are people of color. Thus people without color are now pitted against people of color, and thus we enter upon a period of racist counter-revolution after a period of racist exploitation.

When a U.S. white man says, "I'd rather be dead than Red," what he really means is that he'd rather be dead than not be boss. White people in the United States still believe that they are the economically most advanced people in the world, but never face the fact that they are the politically most backward people in the world. They think that they should decide the way other countries develop just as they think they should decide when and if black people inside the United States should or should not advance.

Right now, they are still in the process of having the cold fact brought home to them that the United States is just one little spot on the total earth, and that insisting on being boss is putting them squarely on a suicidal course. Korea was the turning point. It was the first place where the great might of the United States and its United Nations-sanctioned allies faced a stand-off because of the entering Chinese troops. The lesson of Korea was conveniently forgotten in 1962 when the late President Kennedy was able to get Russia to back down in the confrontation over missile placements in Cuba. Russia's backdown regenerated characteristic American arrogance, which was further encouraged by the accelerating ideological conflict between Russia and China. It was very clear that the Russians were ready to put their own domestic development first, over and above any consideration of the need of the world revolutionary forces in the developing countries to accelerate their revolution and to achieve both political and economic freedom from United States domination and exploitation. Thus encouraged, the United States plunged headfirst into the Vietnam war in order to prove to the French and to themselves that no people of color could defeat people without color. They saw the Chinese Communists challenging their domination of Asia, despite the fact that it was United States air forces, missile bases, naval bases, etc., which completely surrounded China, and despite the fact that the Chinese had not built up any substantial force of hydrogen bombs, missiles, or polaris submarines to threaten the United States.

Vietnam has been the turning point for the counter-revolution. Asia was to be thrust back by massive military force into its place as a colonially subjected section of the world, just as Africa had been thrust back by subversion and intrigue. The United States policy was borrowed from Machiavelli's *Prince*. In that book, a foreign force is invited in by the alleged leaders of a country to kill off the opposition. The foreign force then does such an effective job of killing off the inhabitants that there is no one left to invite him to leave. In this way the invited guest is liberated to pursue his wholesale take-over of the country. The United States went Machiavelli one better. It put together a government and then sent this government to Saigon to join up with a puppet leader. Then the puppet leader was assassinated and another puppet installed who would owe not only allegiance, but his very life and future existence to the United States.

But there were two traps in this supposedly well-made scheme. First of all, in this day and age the weaker the puppet, the more demands he puts on the foreign ruler to whom he owes his very existence; thus the foreign ruler is drawn deeper and deeper into the game and must play the hand dealt out by the puppet rather than deal out the cards. Second, the Vietnamese people, North and South, were not the Africans or the Latin Americans or the black Americans the United States had always been able to divide and rule.

Having fought the French and forced them to come to the Geneva Conference, the Vietnamese people were not going to stand by and see their victorious struggle for freedom and self-determination turned into defeat by the United States. The U.S. had also miscalculated the stage of development of the world revolution. Instead of old allies and colonially subjected nations flocking to its side and sending in their forces to be the shock troops preparing for a triumphal United States entry at the last moment (as in the two world wars), all the United States has been able to involve have been some forces from its South Korean and Thailand lackeys and from white Australia, which is the South Africa of Asia.

Who, then, was to be the cannon fodder? The black youth for whom the United States no longer had any use because mechanization, automation, and cybernation had already made them obsolete; the poor white trash whose hatred for black people far exceeded their ambition to struggle to improve their own poor living conditions; and other youth who, after long periods of interrupted employment for their parents, were only now able to think of going to colleges and universities.

The first two groups, black youth and poor white trash, were the original recruits. Black youth who could not find employment joined the armed services rather than starve in the streets or be turned into welfare beggars and street hustlers and petty criminals. White trash joined because they had little education or ambition but plenty of zest for authority over others, and the armed forces were the perfect place for them to realize a sense of power, particularly when they were to serve as occupation forces in Africa, Asia, and Latin America. For many of these, the Confederate flag became a symbol in Vietnam, partly to affront the black troops serving beside them and partly out of a nostalgia for the bossism of the past, when they had lorded it over black males and females.

The white college youth, however, had neither the reasons nor the needs and ambitions of either of the other two strata and thus was from the beginning a reluctant force. Seizing upon the fact that the Selective Service Act provides various openings for legal deferment, such as attendance in school, physical standards, and moral and conscientious objection, the students used these to protect themselves from being drafted. Then, as each escape valve was barred by draft directors who were aware of the mechanism being used, the students were forced to deepen and accelerate their anti-draft movement. This acceleration came at a time when the old pacifist movement was beginning to recede: having gone through a long period of fighting to ban the bomb, it was confused and disoriented by agreements between Russia and the United States on the issue of nuclear testing. These old-time pacifists gave the students some support and encouragement in their draft resistance, but the students went far beyond them. They began to take over the university campuses, challenging the right of college administrations to undertake various military research projects on behalf of the government, or to permit military and industrial establishments to recruit on the campuses. In this way, the students began to map out a struggle for themselves, outside the black movement, in which their own survival and not just their sympathies for others were involved. And in this way, the student movement not only questioned the role of the United States in Vietnam, but began to challenge the total role of the United States power structure as an imperialist and counter-revolutionary force at home and abroad. Out of this challenge came reactions from the segment of the population which accepts the official policies of the military and industrial establishments as best for the country, and out of these reactions came counter-demonstrations.

The counter-demonstrations were mainly aimed at the students, indicting them not only for their specific political views but also for their general style of life, which is so contrary to accepted middle-class standards.

Student activity steadily gained support from all over the world—from England, Sweden, France, Italy, Japan. By contrast, the counter-demonstrations, lacking any positive perspective or even any conviction of ultimate victory, served to expose the United States' international isolation from all but those tied to it for total financial sustenance. This lack of support for the counter-revolutionary demonstrators by masses of people elsewhere in the world, as well as the growing signs of the break-up of the old Western alliance, have cast doubts into the counter-revolutionary movement. Why has there been no real support from England, France, etc.? Why should "we help them if they don't help us in time of crisis?" "Didn't we bail them out after World War II?" France, in particular, has come in for loud denunciation as a traitor to the "Free World" (i.e., to neo-colonialism). Not only have these questions not brought satisfactory answers, but they have created further doubts about the ability of the United States to mobilize support of its policies and have thereby increased doubts as to its ability to win in the traditional United States style.

Unaccustomed to the strategy and tactics of the Vietnamese in warfare, and organized on the basis of massive firepower which requires either a stationary foe or stabilized lines from which to launch offensives, the United States has become dependent upon massive airpower for saturation bombing not only of enemy supply lines and the enemy population but even in close combat between United States forces and Vietnamese forces. Airpower is used by the United States as a substitute for infantry. But sheer airpower cannot ferret out a constantly mobile foe, nor can it occupy land or territory. Since Vietnam is not just a little country, U.S. occupation would require manpower on a scale far beyond its present mobilization and this at a time when it is not only being deserted by its erstwhile allies but when the revolutionary forces all over the world are on the upsurge, requiring the United States to have at hand innumerable garrisons of troops ready to take off for places all over the globe.

Until 1966 black people in the United States had not been very vocal in their denunciation of the war in Vietnam. On the whole they stayed out of anti-war demonstrations because they believed that their struggle was for civil rights. Blacks in this country have from the very beginning been uncertain whether integration was possible or not. On every issue, international or national, the average black person is torn between wanting to be a part of this country and being repelled by its policies. It has taken the steady and brutal rejection of the black man by white society in the course of the civil rights struggle to help clarify his thoughts. That is why, even though the black man has felt an identity with people of color all over the world and even to a considerable extent appreciated the similarity between their colonization and his, he has come later to his vocal and aggressive opposition to the war in Vietnam than have white students. However, with the upsurge of the Black Power movement and with the recriminations against blacks at home for this movement, black people have begun to recognize the racist character of U.S. wars abroad. The wave of rebellion which erupted in the streets in Watts in 1965 and exploded in Detroit in 1967 has been the basis for deepening the consciousness in the black movement nationally and internationally.

Nationally, black youths began to see more clearly how they have been produced as cannon fodder for the war abroad by the systematic racism at home that refuses to educate and upgrade them. Internationally, they have come to recognize that their struggle for power at home has more in common with the struggle of the United States' enemies than it has with the people of the United States. The underlying assumption of United States' invincibility against a less well-armed foe also began to be questioned by blacks as they witnessed the mobilization of thousands of armed troops to quell their own almost totally disarmed forces. All this has helped them to see how only their full support could give the United States the necessary manpower to continue.

Now that support from black youth is split, a rising tide of struggle against the draft is taking many forms, often with the desperate cunning of the Vietnamese in battle.

With resistance to the war growing at home, the President is seeking some kind of settlement. But whatever settlement he has in mind, it is not the kind which can hold the world revolution in check or which the revolution can accept with any kind of finality. Finality for the United States would mean the establishment of a status quo or of stable areas under its influence and control. But this stability is no longer possible. Indeed, the tenacity of the Vietnamese has drawn the United States deeper and deeper into a trap, the kind of trap that makes impossible the stand-off sought and achieved for some years in Korea. And even if this kind of stand-off were possible, the United States itself cannot support too many of these Korean truces, because each one requires the pouring out of United States resources without commensurate economic return.

This lack of economic return is beginning to upset the economic and industrial sector of the country, despite the tremendous profits it is making off the nation's military adventures abroad. Thus the economic and industrial sector has begun to clamor for some kind of settlement. But even as it does, the hysteria of grass-roots fascist forces mounts for all-out victory. An all-out victory, however, requires an all-out war. An all-out war requires an attack not just on Vietnam but on China. An attack on China means a declaration of war and a declaration of war in the modern world comes not in words but by the dropping of the Bomb. The dropping of the Bomb is a suicidal course because the United States is vulnerable to the Bomb as only a highly concentrated industrialized country can be.

The gap today between the dispossessed of the world and the possessors (i.e., the neo-colonialists) is far wider than was the gap between the feudalists and the capitalists several hundred years ago. A rising tide of capitalism made possible the emergence of a new class which began to control territories and peoples hitherto ruled by royalist monarchs and aristocrats. The rule of the feudalists had been primarily over land and the agricultural produce from that land. Capitalism introduced the technological revolution into production. Its very organization of production required a fluid and growing labor force, a labor force not only regimented and organized by production but able to use this organization as a means to press demands to improve conditions. However, the benefits derived from this organization and pressures still left control, both political and economic, remaining in the hands of the capitalists.

From its very inception, communism has professed theoretically and ideologically, even if it has not always realized its intention practically, that its aim is to use this highly developed technology for the many rather than for a few at the expense of the many. That communism has not completely realized this goal can to some degree be traced to the very underdevelopment or backwardness of the countries in which the communist revolutions have taken place. Those communist nations who are at a stage beyond will have to be judged in the future on the basis of certain standards:

1. How do they relate to other nations who have not reached the same stage and who are struggling against colonial and neocolonial domination?

2. How rapidly are they moving toward socialization of the widest strata of the population and the utilization of technological advances for the further socialization of their people?

3. How much do they encourage the permanent revolution at home and in relation to the masses abroad?

At this stage only China is acting out this role in a nearly complete manner, and in this respect it is the new international center for the revolution, just as the United States is the international center for the counter-revolution. We cannot be certain that all future revolutions will be purely communist in nature or structure. Only one thing is sure: they cannot be feudal or capitalist. To succeed they must start with a maximum mobilization of the masses in order to establish control over all economic, political, and social institutions. Capitalism can no longer question the existence of strong communist nations, except by an insane refusal to face reality, an insanity produced by its inability to reconcile itself with a world revolution with which it cannot coexist.

It is impossible to predict the future, but at the same time those who can anticipate the course of history can help decide it. The feudal lords could not anticipate capitalism. The capitalists cannot or will not anticipate communism. The question is whether any Americans can anticipate the direction which the dispossessed of the world will take.

The answer will come in this century as the war between the races expands and deepens. In this war the very question of the existence of man is at stake. Land, goods, production are important stages in the development of man. But today the world revolution is not over these things. It is over man.

The Vietnamese struggle does not by any means rid the world of capitalism, colonialism, or neo-colonialism, the byproduct of capitalism. But the Vietnamese people represent and reveal the beginning of its final disintegration. Not even the Bomb can restore it to world domination. The future belongs to the dispossessed of the world.

*1968*

# The Labor Movement: Revolutionary or——

On May 1, 1965, a few months after Malcolm X's assassination, a group of black militants met in Detroit and founded the Organization for Black Power. The founding statement called for blacks to organize the cities in the same way the factories had been organized by labor in the 1930's. Blacks "must struggle to control, to govern the cities, as workers struggled to control and govern the factories of the 30's," the statement read.

In *The American Revolution* I traced the decline of organized labor from a movement which had launched the productive forces of this highly advanced society on the road of control of production to an organization which had not only allowed itself to be incorporated into the system but more often than not had rushed to the defense of the system in order to control the militancy of the workers. Today, organized labor, which once was a movement, does not move except in support of the Establishment. Its relationship to the Establishment, industrial and political and military, is that of a force which accepts the American capitalist system as the best in the world and believes it need only be reformed and refined to give workers a bigger share of the pie. Thus, when management offers labor a profit-sharing plan, this does not bother organized labor at all. Its only uncertainty revolves around the question of whether management will really declare large enough dividends to compensate for low wages. Organized labor will take its share any way it can get it, so long as it gets its share. Getting one's share is a unique United States phenomenon which is organically tied to the other unique United States phenomenon of constantly climbing up the social ladder and bettering oneself at the expense of those beneath. This specific United States way of life has been made possible by the fact that this country, unlike any other country in the world, has had inside it a colonized people, the black work force, disciplined by slavery and constantly kept at the bottom of the social ladder to do the dirtiest work and take the cast-off jobs, homes, and schools abandoned by others as they climb up the ladder.

Until World War II the industrial work force of the United States consisted chiefly of immigrants from Europe who came to escape their regimented and impoverished lives with a vision of America as a land where you could rise from rags to riches in a few years. With this view of the land they were coming to, it was to be expected that they would find acceptable the view of black people held by the whites already in the country. Regardless of the fact that these workers carried on and had to carry on militant struggles against the American capitalists, their struggle was always limited by their acceptance of a social stratum in the United States which was not only kept beneath them by the system but which they were willing to keep down themselves as a basis for their own elevation.

The labor movement of the 1930's had in it these people, who were either immigrants or the sons of immigrants. Although they struggled against capitalism, they were at the same time enjoying the fruits of American capitalism's unique racist system.

Today, as the threat of upheaval from the force at the bottom of the ladder increases, the most rabid supporters of the system are the last immigrants who came from Europe, mainly the Polish, Slavic, and Italian workers. They are rabid in their support because they were the last to be really accepted into the United States' family circle. Only since World War II have the Italian people become Italians rather than "Wops" or "Dagoes," and the Polish people Poles instead of "Polacks." These are the people who feel most threatened by the black revolt. Ironically, until the civil rights struggle moved to the North only a few years ago, many blacks up North, where most Italians are congregated, thought the Italians had more in common with them, in dress, in behavior, in social atmosphere, etc., than any other immigrant group. Yet today it is where Italians live most closely to blacks that the violence between the two is most explosive.

It is true that the immigrant's feeling about blacks is not wholly of his own making. From the moment he arrives in the country, he is not only told about black inferiority but is able to observe how every other ethnic group rules over and abuses blacks.

When one speaks of the labor movement, it is necessary to realize that the movement was primarily a Northern movement and that organized labor never really could or would tackle the question of the division of labor in the South. Only in the mines and mills, where the ethnic structure was already firmly entrenched, did labor organize in the South.

In the early days of civil rights legislation the labor movement, particularly its national leadership and the CIO wing, fought for such bills as anti-poll tax, anti-lynching, etc. This legislation had little concrete meaning for the rank-and-file Northern worker, so he supported it passively and without protest. In the early days of the King movement in the South, union locals would even send donations to the Southern movement, usually under the influence of the few socially conscious radicals from the thirties who were still in or around the movement.

Today the labor organizations are as streamlined as management in business. University experts plan wage and security strategy and a few workers work their way up through the political machine which the union oils in the same way all U.S. political machines are oiled. Organized labor is more concerned with saving the union bureaucracy—a small power structure in itself—than with mobilizing workers for political and social struggle, domestic and foreign. Now and then self-righteous statements about civil rights come out from the bureaucracy's office, but the union newspapers are mainly full of stories on social security, pension, and other gains. The labor leaders act as statesmen rather than leaders.

This does not mean that if the socially conscious radicals had not been purged, the labor organization could have been different. Not even the most radical whites ever seriously dreamed of blacks becoming such a social force that they would be demanding changes far beyond labor's wildest dreams.

In *The American Revolution* I said that if it had been possible to incorporate the black work force into production and into the labor movement around 1948, it might have been possible to visualize the integration of the races in the United States. This was mere speculation. For when blacks themselves began to struggle outside the labor apparatus, their struggle began to test and strain the labor unions.

The first serious test came with the burning of the buses in Anniston, Alabama, when labor was challenged to send mixed loads of black and white workers into the South. Labor responded with a donation rather than confront the ranks with an action.

In 1963 the Birmingham crisis erupted in the industrial city of Birmingham and moved the black struggle up North. In the North blacks were mainly concentrated in the cities, with more unemployed than in the South. Although government and industry had made room in the labor force for the refugees from the 1956 Hungarian revolt, they had made no similar attempt for blacks. Black people were still regarded as scavengers who had to pick up the leavings that other ethnic groups had discarded.

The black demands for changes up North also carried with them the demand for serious economic changes, while in the South the demands were for social changes, chiefly in public accommodations—to be able to eat in a restaurant, sit in a park, drink water at a public fountain, ride anywhere on a train, bus or plane, sit on a jury, etc. Although blacks up North did not enjoy all these rights, they had the illusion that they were there to be taken or enjoyed. With the unfolding of their demands, however, they found themselves opposed, not only by the South but by white Northerners.

The unions were in a contradiction from this moment onward. Every time blacks demanded job opportunities, the unions could only say they were on record favoring equal opportunity but it was up to management and the government to provide jobs. They preferred to emphasize that the government should stimulate more jobs, even make-believe ones like the WPA of the 1930's, for as long as the emphasis was put on government or management, the union did not have to confront its own membership (primarily white at this point). To confront its members meant one job less for a white worker. Rather than advocate the concept that if all suffered alike, they would find grounds for struggling together, the union catered to its white members. A few black workers in the labor organizations raised this issue, but the union did not support them or allow the issue to be pushed to a decision. Instead, it let the wrath of the white worker simmer and grow. The older black workers inside the union had also become passive and complacent and to this day have not been a serious factor either in the labor organizations or in the black movement. The old black workers are as conservative as the old white ones are reactionary.

When the word "reactionary" is used to describe the white workers, it is a mild description. It describes them in the same language as the unions use to describe management and the Republican Party. The AFL is dominated by construction and transportation workers, carpenters, brick masons, electricians, sheet metal and iron workers, painters, etc. Its membership is arrogantly hostile to black workers. The leadership is comfortable with the counter-revolution both at home and abroad. Even supporting United States foreign policy is not enough. It goes beyond this in its demands for counter-revolution abroad. It is as much anti-communist as it is pro-fascist. The AFL workers, spurred on by their leaders, have become the stoutest supporters of the Vietnam war and antagonists of demonstrating pacifists and students. They are as ready to storm and stomp them as the Nazis were to stomp the socialists in the early days of Hitler.

The UAW and CIO unions do not lead or urge their members to act against but rather to support the war effort. Then, in their attempt to maintain a liberal image, they associate with allegedly liberal politicians. The liberal politician in the United States is like the conservative in Europe and the conservative or right-wing politician in the United States is like a European fascist. The worker in the United States is more conservative than either the politician or the industrial leader, except when questions of pay are involved. While the industrialists or big capitalists are recognizing the impact and implications of the black movement, nationally and internationally, the workers are growing more fascist in nature every day. They see every development of the black movement as a direct threat to themselves in the same vicious fashion as the colonialists in Africa and Asia see the colonized people.

Fascism in the United States is therefore unique in that it is grass roots rather than from the top down. Today the Minute Men, America Firsters, White Citizens' Councils, and the scores of other white organizations organized to defend the United States from the demands of the blacks for justice are made up of workers, skilled and unskilled, who work every day alongside blacks in the shop and then night after night organize in the suburbs against these same blacks.

Sometimes they will admit to some black workers with whom they have long worked that they are not against them but rather against those guerrillas and jitterbugs in the black ghetto. They have no sense of understanding or concern that these black jitterbugs or guerrillas are the sons of the workers in whom they are confiding or that even these old passive blacks are being educated by white antagonism into becoming guerrillas themselves. Like the white elements of the lumpen who have found a place to express their bossism and the sense of power in the army, these white workers see blacks as threatening their very jobs when their jobs are in fact being threatened by automation and cybernation. Rather than accept automation as technical progress and demand a right to a livelihood regardless of its utilization by management, they choose to try to ward off the blacks not only on the job market but even in their antagonism to black control of the black community, which offers no threat to them. Often afraid to confront the blacks at the point of production, they organize outside to inflame not only the other white workers but other strata of the population not engaged in the process of production. Side by side with the development of the black revolutionary forces grows the white workers' counter-revolutionary force.

Today as the police force of every major city is rapidly growing into a garrison of occupation forces, the chief supporters of the "Support Your Local Police" movement are the working classes. Wherever there is a new community that consciously excludes blacks on the basis of race (as distinct from those bourgeois communities which exclude on the basis of economics), the community is composed of workers. In every major urban center there is a suburban community which is notorious for its exclusion of blacks. In Detroit this is Dearborn, which is composed mainly of Polish workers who fled from Hamtramck, once the largest Polish settlement outside of Warsaw, Poland. Dearborn's residents are refugees from the threat of the increasing encirclement of Hamtramck by black people. Dearborn's mayor is elected year after year on the slogan "Keep Dearborn Clean"— meaning "clean" of black people. Chicago has its Cicero, where Italian workers keep Cicero clean of black people. Cleveland has both a Slavic and an Italian section, where pitched battles take place periodically between blacks and whites. These two ethnic groups stand out, but they only reflect outwardly what is deeply imbedded in every ethnic group of the white working class.

"White working class" is not a class description in the classical European sense, because white workers are by the very nature of U.S. development and history a class above all blacks. The blacks are an under-class which has developed despite the fact that they have been systematically damned by the system. "The worker" supports the system because of his special position in an upper class even when he is in poverty or at some points worse off than blacks.

Of all the classes in the United States "the workers" feel more threatened by blacks than anyone else. Today the worst that could happen would be the arming of these workers. In fact, they are already arming themselves at such an alarming rate that even the power structure is deeply disturbed by the fascist trend among workers who may turn on those in power. At this stage they are content to turn their hate and frustration on the blacks who disturb their domestic tranquillity and also challenge the white male domination which has flattered and fattened their egos as conquering beings.

Whenever and wherever possible, these workers join certain forces, such as the police or National Guard, the Special Forces, etc., in order to be in a position to help keep the blacks in their place in case of emergency.

Blacks in the United States have long since by-passed the labor organizations. No one knows this better than the labor leaders, who cannot relate to the young blacks either inside or outside the labor force and find the few old blacks they have incorporated into their political machines of little use in trying to relate to young blacks. Younger blacks are extremely sensitive to the antagonism of white workers and cannot distinguish them from oppressors.

Already in Detroit, home-base for the UAW-CIO and for Walter Reuther, labor's most progressive spokesman, young black workers are rallying to DRUM (Dodge Revolutionary Union Movement). DRUM is made up of young black production workers who have organized local groups inside the Ford and GM plants after a series of successful wildcat strikes at the Chrysler-Hamtramck plant. The League of Revolutionary Black Workers is the organization of these new black workers, and their allegiance is to the black community, not to organized labor. Unlike the older black workers, who were grateful for any jobs, these younger men believe that their confinement to the old back-breaking jobs on the production line is strictly a manifestation of the racism of American society. From their point of view, these jobs, no matter how much they pay, are no better than the field-hand jobs their slave forefathers were forced to perform in the South. What the union and an older generation of workers accept as the company's prerogative, these young blacks challenge. To them, the statement that the "company has the sole right to run the plant as it sees fit" expresses not a truth but a popular prejudice.

The demands and the expectations of these young black workers far exceed the wildest dreams of the labor movement and of earlier generations of workers even in their most militant days. The white workers who monopolize the skilled jobs—plumbers, electricians, tool-and-die men, machine repairmen—think only in terms of more money per hour. The DRUM member, at the bottom of the production ladder, demands the hiring of black plant doctors, fifty black foremen, and even a black chairman for the Board of Directors. He is not satisfied with any old job; he wants control of the plant itself.

Inside the plant, white workers are being shaken up, not just by these demands but by the fact that older black workers who once seemed so docile are becoming increasingly sympathetic and even supportive of the young blacks, thus threatening the peaceful coexistence between white and black inside the plant that was once so comforting to the white workers.

Since white racism is expressing itself at the present time most clearly in the white work force and since black nationalism is regarded by the white worker as his chief antagonist, a clash is inevitable. This clash is being held off only because squarely between these two forces are the military forces, either in the form of police or National Guard or state troopers or the U.S. army. Up to now all forces have been primarily aimed at crushing the blacks, while the whites have been either relieved or content with the result. The labor leaders cannot resolve this potential clash because, like the government and political structure, they have waited too long, letting the whites go their merry and not so merry way, joining the system, supporting the system, until today if they are not the system of racism itself, they are its main prop.

In the United States, the alienation of man from man started long before the alienation of man in production. It is this alienation that black and white of the lowest strata will bleed from most.

*1968*

# Civil Rights Legislation

Every year in the U.S. Senate or House of Representatives there is a bill or bills called a "civil rights bill," generally initiated by some senator, congressman, or even the President, which has as its aim the quieting or pacification of black unrest. Sometimes it comes after a revolt, sometimes in anticipation of a revolt. For whatever reason it is always clear before the ink is even dry on the final document that it will not be sufficient and that next session there will have to be another civil rights bill introduced.

It will not be sufficient because in the course of the debate over the bill the views of the government and the white mass clearly indicate to the black mass that the bill is just another search for a means of pacification, with white Americans still having the power to decide just what rights blacks should have and what rights blacks should not have.

United States citizens, particularly white citizens, were either pleased or displeased by the recent report issued by the President's commission to study and evaluate the causes of last summer's rebellion, known as the Kerner report. They were pleased if they accepted the commission's findings of racism in white America, U.S.A. They were displeased if they disagreed with the findings or if they thought nothing would be done about them.

However, pleasure or displeasure is not the issue. What is important is that when one seriously examines the analysis and the recommendations we find a total contradiction between them.

The analysis says that white racism is the cause of the explosions. The recommendations propose programs to cure the black man who is the victim of this racism. There are no programs devoted to serious prescriptions to cure or check white racism. Essentially the cures prescribed (housing, education, and employment) apply to blacks as if they were the ones who are in need of cures.

If the report had dealt with police brutality and arrived at the conclusion that police brutality was responsible for the rebellions, the logical recommendation would have been some prescription for a fundamental change in the behavior of policemen and the police department. Or if an investigation had proved that blacks themselves had been responsible, then the natural and logical conclusion would have been some kind of prescription, punishment, or reward for black people.

Yet so irresponsible and illogical are the American people and those whom they elect to represent them both locally and nationally that, having decided where the responsibility for a rebellion lies, they don't even think of doing something to or about those responsible. It is like saying that the way to keep white sheriffs, policemen, Ku Klux Klansmen, White Citizens' Councilmen, Minutemen, Birchites, and other American fascists from lynching any more blacks is to put the blacks to work, send them to school, and build some new housing developments in the ghetto.

Nothing is said about a crusade to wipe out racism, either by taking away power from racists (i.e., the whites in this society), which is the most logical remedy, or at the very least a crash program to re-educate whites, adults, youth, policemen, authorities, and the lawmakers who make the laws.

Simultaneous with the report we had the allegedly new "civil rights bill." Any serious examination of this bill would have to conclude that instead of a new civil rights bill, we have a bill to deny civil rights. It has been noted that it is a compromise between the conservative and the liberal forces (i.e., the white forces) in Congress. It is just that, a typical white compromise similar to the Great Compromise of 1877 whereby the Northern industrialists made a deal with the South which would allow the South to re-enslave the allegedly freed blacks for cheap labor as long as the North could proceed to industrialize and bring in immigrant labor from abroad.

The new civil rights bill allegedly gives blacks the right to buy or rent in what have been off-limit neighborhoods, providing that public announcement has been made that a vacancy exists. If, however, it should happen that black people in Illinois, Michigan, Alabama, Georgia, Mississippi, etc., should be abused by the white racism which is now officially admitted to exist and if the black people in any of these states should invite a black brother to come in and help them organize some form of resistance, these brothers can then be charged with inciting a rebellion or riot.

So for the sake of an empty right to make inquiries about a vacant house or apartment without being bluntly told that it is not for rent or sale to black people (as is now the practice), white liberals have legally bartered away to white fascists the political and social right of black people to freedom of movement.

Thus while one committee of the government charges that it is white racism which causes blacks to rebel, another body elected by the people who are admittedly white racists writes into law a Bill of White Racism.

This contradiction is nothing new in the United States. In *The American Revolution,* I pointed out that the American people have evaded taking political responsibility for so long that the question of what is right and what is wrong completely evades them, day-in and day-out and especially in times of crisis. They have been leaving politics to the politicians. So today when they are confronted by the second civil war, a war which is clearly between one set of people (black) and another set of people (white), they cannot and will not recognize that until some whites are ready to struggle against, instead of compromising with, some whites over which way this society should go, the struggle between whites and blacks will continue and intensify.

What is particularly lacking in white analysis, what whites fail to recognize and what is at the heart of the concept of Black

Power, is that a social force has grown up in this society that is in fundamental antagonism to this society, thus making conflict and violence inevitable.

To recognize this antagonism would mean that these whites would have to recognize that no new set of laws or bills passed by this constitutional body will or can be the basis for a solution. For what is at stake is the Constitution itself.

Few blacks have said this, but the fact that they have not said it is not important. What is important is that by their actions and general indifference to new legislation, they have shown their underlying conviction that there is something wrong with the institution of Congress itself. While Congress is debating, black people are constantly carrying out activities which nullify or amend all existing or to be written laws.

At the heart of the issue is the fact that Congress does not and cannot represent black people. It cannot because Congress is motivated by the concept that the Constitution is sound and only needs to be amended, when in fact the Constitution was written on the premise that black people were not even people, let alone citizens. Now that blacks are engaged in a revolutionary struggle, the constitution by which the United States is finally governed will have to be a revolutionary constitution based upon the new social forces, just as the Constitution of 1787 was a constitution based upon the new social forces of that day. A revolution does not develop unless the government has been unable to resolve the basic issues under the existing framework. Today most of the blacks are in the cities. They are being driven there by the mechanization of the farm and by the techniques of expulsion used by white Southerners who feel threatened by their potential political power to take over the rural areas of the South. They have been lured to the city by the industrial revolution and two world wars, and by the belief that city life is far superior to rural existence. But in the city the revolutions of automation and cybernation are making them expendable or obsolete.

The present Constitution was geared to the power of the states at a time when the states were able to meet the needs of the people. This was in the agricultural era when most people were on the farms and had relatively few needs except roads to the markets in the cities. Today the social forces have all shifted to the city and only one out of every eighteen citizens is on the farm. The cities' needs go far beyond any needs envisaged in the Constitution or the state apparatus set up to fulfill these needs.

*1968*

# King, Malcolm, and the Future of the Black Revolution

A few days ago Dr. Martin Luther King was gunned down in Memphis, Tennessee, where for the second time in less than two weeks he was getting ready to lead a united black community in a march to demonstrate support of the garbage workers. The garbage workers of Memphis, like those throughout the South, are predominantly black, and 40 percent of their number could qualify for welfare rolls on the basis of their pay.

For nearly two months the Memphis garbage workers had been on strike for union recognition and better pay and working conditions. The key issue was union recognition, which the city administration refused because that would mean recognizing the right of blacks to organize their power. The mayor, in fact, had been elected by whites, in a city that is about 40 percent black, on a program for keeping the blacks in their place ("law and order"). On February 25 he had created the official climate for crushing any struggles by black people by violence when he refused to negotiate with the garbage workers and had the police beat and spray with MACE the black citizens of Memphis, 1,000 strong, who had come to the city council chambers to demonstrate their support of the garbage workers.

During the first march some relatively minor violence had erupted when youngsters broke windows and hurled bricks, and the police had immediately over-reacted by clubbing and tear-gassing peaceful marchers. The excessive counter-violence and the subsequent bringing in of the National Guard gave further official encouragement to counter-revolutionary assassins.

King was murdered in the presence of over 150 policemen and other witnesses. The white man who was seen dropping a rifle and fleeing after the shooting has as of this date not been apprehended, or if he has been, the fact has not been made public. During the weekend following King's brutal murder, blacks erupted in over 100 cities. Scores of these cities were set to the torch, and many of them were then put under military occupation and dusk-to-dawn curfews reminiscent of the blackouts of Britain and occupied Europe during World War II. National Guardsmen, state police, and federal troops patrolled the streets in caravans of police cars and tanks—even in a city like Detroit, where the number of fires had been less than that during routine periods. A national crisis existed.

Since the Watts rebellion of 1965 there has been more warfare between blacks and the authorities, spontaneously erupting over incidents of police brutality or cold-blooded killings, than during the two years preceding the first Civil War. Each and every eruption could be traced to some overt or covert form of brutality by some facet of U.S. authority or by some white fascist who knew he had white official support. King's assassination, whether it came from those opposed to his support of a local black community or his stand on the Vietnam war (the difference being only one of national or international racism), has broken the last link of the chain binding whites and blacks. When or if some new link will be forged remains to be decided by the historical development of the struggle.

In assessing the reason why King was murdered, it is not important that King was the leader of a non-violent movement. King is dead because he acted, and as every schoolboy knows Plato talked and no one cared, but Socrates acted and was driven to his death. Realizing that this brutal murder has broken the last link between blacks and whites, the white power structure from the President's office down through governors, mayors, and liberals has co-opted King in order to emphasize his strategy of

non-violence and belief in the legislative process and the fundamental redeemability of whites. They are trying to convince the
black people that this is the only way to black liberation. The
murder of King and of the scores of other blacks who adopted
King's approach is disproof of their every utterance.

On the other hand, the murder of Malcolm, who refused to
restrict the movement to non-violence and had no illusions about
the white man, demonstrates that it is not enough just to repeat
Malcolm's famous dictum of "by all means necessary," as so
many black nationalists do. The most important issue is not violence or non-violence. The black movement in this country will
continue to pay the heavy price of assassination of its leaders until
it has enough power to establish its own law and order in specific
areas. The issue is whether and when the movement can build an
organization strong enough to struggle by all means necessary to
win this power, sometimes violently, sometimes non-violently,
sometimes retreating, sometimes attacking, sometimes on the defensive, sometimes on the offensive, but always retaining sufficient
initiative to maintain a momentum toward its objective of power,
deciding what it can achieve at each stage of the struggle in
terms of its goals and objectives just as any military general in
war sizes up his opponents and elects when to fight and when
not to fight.

A revolution is not just constant fighting. There are times when
it is necessary to develop the cadre and the people by engaging
them in certain political struggles to advance their knowledge
and develop their talent for engaging the enemy as well as for
leading not-as-yet-engaged sections of the community into the
fray to strengthen its social force. In fact, the rhetoric of the black
movement today is far beyond its leaders' capacity to produce.
This rhetoric not only exceeds the movement's organizational
strength and structure to implement. It also tends to disguise the
lack of clarity as to the kind of Black Power which blacks are
seeking. For this reason alone the movement has and will continue for some time to take the form of spontaneous eruptions.

To evaluate King one has to look back to where today's struggle
started, keeping in mind that all revolutions start with demands
for reform by an oppressed group. If those demands are granted,

the movement may stop and the period is called a "reformation." However, if the demands of the reform movement are not granted or if they do not achieve what the people interpret them to mean, the people usually go on beyond and make a revolution, recognizing that only by taking power from those in power can they make the changes and achieve the rights that they have come to believe are theirs.

When Mrs. Rosa Parks refused to yield her seat in the front of the bus thirteen years ago in Montgomery, Alabama, she did what no black in the South had done since Reconstruction and what none of today's black militants in the North would have done if they had been in the South at that time. For that, if nothing more, Mrs. Parks is the mother of the present-day struggle.

Martin Luther King was pushed into the leadership of the movement because he was young and because he had not antagonized any of the old Southern preachers who, like their Northern counterparts, were serving the white power structure by pacifying black workers and domestics on Sundays so that they could be ready to go back to work on Monday and endure another week of indignities and brutalities. The community thought he could work between the preachers and the people, never recognizing that he would go far beyond their wildest dreams.

In the weeks and months following his baptism to the wrath of the white racist—the bombing of his home, the police harassment, the efforts to sabotage the struggle by the courts—King caught the imagination of black people, both North and South. Up North there was not a single one of today's black nationalist leaders and militants who did not feel a relation to King's movement, if he was old enough at the time. Any militant old enough to attend a rally sang "We shall overcome" with as much fervor as any of King's followers in the South. For in this period no Northerners were carrying on any serious struggle. The Muslims, who had been developing a philosophy of blackness, were only active internally. Other nationalists dreamed of going back to Africa "some day." There were some blacks up North working in the Fair Employment Practices committees of the labor movement, but none of these old labor activists had advanced even as far as King.

There can be no question that King's movement was a reform movement and that it had as its intent the reformation of white people. His philosophy was one which could have been revolutionary in the sense of displacing those in power only if it had been developed in a country like India, where the oppressed were the overwhelming majority struggling against a small colonialist ruling minority. An oppressed minority, however, can win only by revolution. Actually, of course, all revolutions are started by minorities who in the course of the struggle either win over or divide the majority sufficiently even if they are all one ethnic grouping.

In the United States blacks are a minority. However, because four-fifths of the world is black and in a revolutionary or pre-revolutionary stage of development, blacks in the United States are not a minority in the usual sense of the word. They are also one of the largest minorities that a country has ever had inside itself. And in the largest cities all over the country they are very close to a majority. Because of their strategic positions, both physically and socio-psychologically, they have the capacity, if organized, to create bases of power for themselves in various areas and at various points of division among the enemy.

King's movement, based as it was on the reclamation of the white man, did not intend to be a revolution. It was revolutionary, nonetheless, in the sense that from its inception it went further in confronting whites and in creating conflict between black and white over issues than any blacks, North or South, had ever dreamed of trying to go before. And even though civil rights are only the normal common rights that a nation should grant to its citizens, the civil rights struggle in this country was a revolutionary struggle because blacks had been denied these normal rights.

Any movement, reformist or revolutionary, has to have concrete objectives, a general strategy to achieve these objectives, and a cadre organized around these. King's movement fulfilled these needs. His objectives or demands consisted of legal guarantees of black people's rights to equal access to public accommodations, to register and vote, and to other forms of civil rights. His offensive strategy was based on the method of confrontation.

Blacks, convinced of the rightness of their demands, confronted whites who either had to yield to these just demands or expose themselves as defenders of the indefensible. His organizational structure was geared to achieve these objectives by this method. True, he also believed that whites could be redeemed through the heroic suffering of black people. Borrowing from Gandhi, his strategy included non-violence, but behind the rhetoric it can be seen that this served mainly as a means of self-discipline among the demonstrators. His cadres were effective because of this discipline, but they were also disciplined by the precision of his objectives, his method of offensive struggle for these objectives, and an organization built around the objectives and offensive methods. His organization brought together clergymen, businessmen, professional men, and students. They raised the money and planned the sit-ins, the campaigns for voter registration, and the innumerable demonstrations by which black communities hacked away at segregationist resistance and lowered the barriers against blacks in the political, economic, and social life of the nation.

Maintaining a continuous offensive, King also had what few black leaders have exhibited up to this date, an instinct for the right time to attack, which is the test for any leader, revolutionary or not. This is reaffirmed by his last act, the move into Memphis to engage in a struggle which the labor movement had ignored because of its racism and because of its fear of antagonizing the political structure, and which the Black Power groups could not help because they have not yet devised a strategy for confrontation in order to create the conflict, and thus the gathering momentum, necessary to a movement.

King's critics of today and yesterday point out that many of King's actions did not achieve results, referring particularly to Albany, Georgia; Birmingham, Alabama; and Chicago, Illinois. This is true, but even in failure King's movement achieved success in that it exposed the brutality of the white power structure and, like the Muslims, gave black people a sense of confidence in themselves and the courage to hack away at the long-held feelings of self-hate, complete frustration, and despair of ever being anything but just "another nigger."

Although history will record King's movement as the most vital in the period of reformation, there are certain things that the revolution owes him. His courage against odds, his sense of timing, and his readiness to assume the political risks that leadership imposes make him the father of the present-day movement. The movement today has gone beyond King and reformation. But in 1955 when others were only talking about leaving the South and boasting of how they would not live down South and how much better off they were up North, King acted by assuming leadership of a struggle which no other black man then dared to lead. For that, history not only will enshrine him but will absolve him of some of his failings. And even after black folks have forgotten what he did for them, they will still remember that he was violently killed by a white man and in the presence of at least 150 police officers.

Northern attempts to apply the strategy and tactics of King in the years after Birmingham had very little to show in the way of success. The miseries of slum life in the black ghetto could not be alleviated by civil rights legislation. Civil rights groups boycotted stores, picketed construction projects, etc., in an effort to get better jobs for blacks. They boycotted segregated schools in protest against inferior education. But the liberal regimes up North did not respond with the same kind of counter-violence which had helped the struggle in the South develop a momentum of its own. Thus the civil rights demonstrations and protests in the North only helped to expose the futility of such methods to achieve any significant progress, and helped to drive the leadership of the movement to the conclusion that blacks must acquire power if they are to change their lives.

This first period of struggle in the North culminated in the assassination of Malcolm in February 1965. Unlike King, Malcolm was killed by a black man, who, however, stated at the trial that he had been paid by someone to do the killing, a question which the prosecutor did not pursue. At Malcolm's funeral, unlike at King's, not one white leader had anything to say; nor were there any white leaders there, even though Malcolm had spoken to white audiences all over the country and many celebrities, particularly TV and radio celebrities, boasted that they were friends of Malcolm's. But whites were not going to lend legitimacy to any of Malcolm's ideas by attending his funeral.

Malcolm had not only come from the Muslim movement. In Detroit in 1963, when he made his famous Grassroots Leadership Conference speech, he had begun to deal with revolution and revolutionary struggles and to place the black revolution, as distinguished from the "Negro revolution" so beloved by whites, in the tradition of the great French and Russian revolutions. The organization to which he belonged, the Nation of Islam, had played a very important role in rehabilitating black people, both those inside the organization and, by its influence, those who did not actually join. But it had not evolved any strategy of struggle to achieve the power necessary for black people to rule themselves in a concrete political manner. To this day the Muslims have not seemed to understand that even the Muslim religion at one time required not only a religious revolution for men's minds but also a tremendous power struggle by Muslim leaders and their followers, just as those dedicated to the Christian religion had to carry out great power struggles and crusades to institute Christianity in the areas where it now prevails.

Today, even more than in the religious era, the struggles for men's minds require concrete struggles for the power to rule over land, goods, and the means by which goods are produced.

Malcolm X's speech to the Grassroots Leadership Conference revealed that it was essentially on this issue of struggle for power that Malcolm was beginning to find life inside the Muslims increasingly difficult. An organizer and revolutionist by temperament, increasingly exposed to political ideas about past and present revolutions in other countries, Malcolm's mind and skills could no longer be contained within the apocalyptic vision of black ascendancy and white denouement of the Black Muslim religion.

Malcolm's political life, though brief, left an ineradicable impact on the black movement and the black masses, because he led the movement out of the stage of civil rights into the stage of struggle for Black Power. Although he was surrounded by intellectuals, he began to arouse the deepest layer of the black mass which, up North in particular, had not seemed interested in participating in the struggle at all. The method he used was that of chiding and even berating them for their self-hate, their acceptance of the white man in the America as their superior, and their efforts to make themselves acceptable to him and to integrate with the white enemy—when all the time they were being systematically segregated and degraded by this enemy.

The phrase "Malcolm said" became the by-word of the black movement soon after Malcolm was ousted from the Muslims for stating publicly that the "chickens have come to roost" in reference to President Kennedy's assassination. In this statement he summed up unforgettably what many blacks were vaguely aware of but had not been able to or had been afraid to articulate. Black people knew, even as they mourned Kennedy, that the Kennedy government had talked about civil rights but had not prosecuted one white person for the killings, beatings, and brutalizations of the blacks engaged in the civil rights struggle. But blacks didn't want to face this fact. Malcolm stated it so that it had to be faced. This is what he was always doing.

Malcolm was fearless in his recognition that the black revolution in the U.S.A. must be linked to the world revolutionary struggle, a fact which civil rights leaders would gingerly approach and then shy away from.

Malcolm recognized that it was necessary for the movement to go beyond civil rights to a revolutionary struggle against the enemy forces which possessed and ruled. He saw that the struggle of black people in the U.S.A.—dispossessed, despised, uprooted from their past culture and robbed of identification with Africa and the rest of the black world—would have to be linked up with the other revolutionary forces in the world and particularly those of Africa. Thus, after his split with Mr. Muhammad, Malcolm made two trips to Africa in order to establish the necessary relations between the national and the international movements. In his efforts to pull together the national and international forces of the black revolution, Malcolm spent much of his time during this period traveling from city to city in the U.S.A. speaking to the national forces, and traveling to Africa speaking to the international forces. Because this period was so short, it is impossible to determine who Malcolm's constituents really were, except that they were the black masses in general. Trying to bridge the gap between the civil rights struggle, which was carrying out action after action in the South and was led primarily by King and SNCC, and the world black revolution, Malcolm did not and could not develop any serious cadre of people to begin to project a strategy for the philosophy and concepts which he was developing.

His now-famous statement, "ballots or bullets," came not from any projected experience or action but as a reflection on what was happening with the voter registration drive being carried on by King and SNCC in the South and with attempts being made in the North, through the Freedom Now Party in Michigan in particular, to get black people to pool their political power by voting black.

Black people up North identified themselves with what Malcolm was saying as he was saying it, in a way that they have identified with no other black leader. But they did not identify with him in any actions. In the period following the split, Malcolm himself insisted that he was an evangelist rather than an organizer. It cannot be said that Malcolm was incapable of organizing. Organizing was one of his great contributions to the Muslims in the years when he was right-hand man to Mr. Muhammad. But his political life outside the Muslims was too brief to enable him to undertake organizational work. He was suspended in November 1963, shortly after President Kennedy's assassination. He began to develop independently early in 1964, and he was slain in February 1965 following his organization of the Organization for Afro-American Unity. In that period, actually lasting less than a year, his contribution was enormous.

Because Malcolm represented and led the transition from civil rights to revolution, his following since his death is ten times greater than it was at any time during his life. Today many old and young, but particularly the young, quote Malcolm in the same way that people in Europe quote Marx and Lenin and people in China quote Mao. Malcolm had put forward a historical concept of revolution in his Grass Roots speech back in 1963 in Detroit. However, after his split the mass media took him over and portrayed him as a pure advocate of violence vs. non-violence. This has made it difficult to make a true evaluation of Malcolm. Take, for example, the statement "ballots or bullets." The phrase contains the concept of alternatives and the concept of escalation. That is to say, if ballots do not work, then there is no alternative but for the masses to take the road of bullets. The mass media, however, for reasons of its own, represented Malcolm as calling only for violence. What Malcolm was in fact explaining was that a revolutionary movement makes demands which meet the needs of the masses for fundamental changes. If these demands are not granted by peaceful means, the revolution must have a strategy for taking them. Thus, having demanded the right to vote, the struggle would have to escalate to the point of seizing power to vote—first by the threat of violence, and then, if that does not work, by actual violence.

The same is true of another of Malcolm's famous statements, "by all means necessary." The phrase has been interpreted to mean only the advocacy of violence. Yet Malcolm was advocating what every great revolutionist has advocated, that the strategy of revolution requires the escalation of demands and actions, stage by stage, in conflict with the enemy, utilizing the whip of the counter-revolution to deepen the conflict and to drive the revolution forward, without stopping at the most extreme actions required to win.

Malcolm never had the opportunity to develop a cadre to carry out or attempt to carry out a strategy. This is what he left for the emerging nationalist movement to do and that is what up to now the nationalists have not done.

Today from coast to coast black nationalists meet in reverence to Malcolm at services memorializing both his death and his birth. They leave these meetings as loose and incoherent as when they came in. They are no clearer than they were at the time of Malcolm's death.

Malcolm's death exposed the one fundamental weakness of the movement; that no serious black cadre-type organization exists, disciplined by a political perspective and capable of developing and carrying out strategy and tactics necessary to implement this perspective. In his brief independent political existence Malcolm sought to create a unity of blacks. But unity in general is abstract or defensive and only an organization made up of those who are conscious of the positive objectives for which unity is necessary can shape unity into united action and give it meaningful offensive form.

When Stokely Carmichael, the leader of SNCC from 1966 to 1967, shouted "Black Power" on a dusty road in Mississippi in June 1966, he did so in a march which had been organized for civil rights. That the words were uttered in such a context does not detract from their significance nor from the significance of Stokely, whose contribution to the movement is already historic. But what does Black Power mean in political and not just psychological terms? The failure to apply itself to this question remains the chief reason why the rapidly growing nationalist tendency has not been able to launch any offensives. Instead, it has been forced to depend upon the spontaneous outbursts of the masses, rebelling against outrages perpetrated by the oppressor. The movement therefore remains fragmented into little groups, locally and nationally, which are more interested in coming together to "rap" (talk) with each other over what Malcolm said or what the "cat on the corner" is doing or might do than they are in developing a strategy to give direction and meaningful confrontation to what the "cat on the corner" is ready to do. Exhibiting more anti-organizational feeling than organization, they refuse to recognize that the prime need of any revolution is a serious disciplined cadre which can give leadership and structure to the needs of the masses through demands that force them into the arena of struggle. Without such a cadre, a leadership is not leading but is always waiting on the masses to react. With such a structure, a leadership is in a position to place before the masses issues and demands and propose strategy and tactics to realize those demands as well as parallel hierarchies to implement them. The refusal of the leadership to recognize this as its specific task leads to a misconception of the role of the masses in revolution and in turn to a strengthening of the anarchistic tendencies that exist in any revolutionary movement.

What the present and potential leadership of the black revolutionary movement needs to recognize is that, as all past historical experience shows, the masses are not always in a state of revolutionary consciousness. Some days they are just going their way trying to eke out an existence; at other times they are passive and cannot be aroused. Usually they are stimulated to erupt as the result of the whip of the counter-revolution. If the masses were a continuing conscious mass, then the revolution would have already been over! The spontaneous eruption is decisive for any revolution in that no successful revolution is possible without it, but the revolutionary leadership and the cadre must be constantly giving leadership, using propaganda and agitation to organize the struggle and to create the momentum of a continuous offensive toward revolutionary objectives. Across the U.S.A. spontaneous eruptions are taking place and will continue to take place, while the counter-revolution is developing its method of containment and repression. Essentially, the method will be constant states of occupation similar to that of Europe under Hitler or of the French army in Algeria before the Algerians won control.

The United States, however, is neither France nor Algeria— where the occupied were the numerical majority. This factor alone requires the Black Power movement to develop a strategy that will build a movement around escalating demands and escalating struggles so that the movement of escalation assumes a momentum of its own. Such a strategy cannot be devised or implemented except by a leadership certain of its political objectives and with a highly disciplined organization to achieve these objectives.

When Black Power took over the center of the stage of the revolution, it was not just a new stage of development. It also required new insights into the positive objectives of the movement different from those defined by King, and a concrete organization to achieve these objectives which Malcolm did not have the time to organize. Black Power now has the responsibility to structure and state its demands and organize its struggles just as King did for his stage of the movement. When a movement moves from a reform stage to a revolutionary stage, it requires not only people who have developed out of the past but a clear concept of the further development of goals and struggles to achieve these goals.

The black movement today must surmount certain political attitudes which have taken root during the period of transition from reform to revolution.

1. First and foremost is the complete emotional rejection of all past strategies and tactics.

2. The failure to develop and clarify the objectives to be struggled for.

3. Anti-organizational attitudes and rigid beliefs in unorganized spontaneous mass eruptions.

4. Failure to analyze scientifically the stage of development of the country so that it will know what objectives are appropriate at this stage in productive, scientific, political, and social institutions, and the kinds of power it must have in order to make the changes necessary in these institutions.

5. Letting their emotions and feelings control and dictate their actions and reactions, which in essence means that the leaders have no belief in or perspective for final victory and therefore are unable to instill such a perspective in the masses.

In his Grassroots speech Malcolm cited the French and Russian revolutions, emphasizing the role of land in these revolutions and its key role in any revolution, with specific reference to the black (as distinguished from Negro) revolution in the United States. The concept of land remained general. It was possible to take it to mean land in the sense of farmlands to be cultivated, or the land of three or five states, or the land which black people presently occupy in the cities and which is commonly referred to as their "turf." Today the tendencies within the Black Power movement can be clasified according to their interpretation of this central concept of land. The separatists or secessionists have adapted Garvey's "back to Africa" concept to mean setting up a separate black nation in certain states, which will be conferred or surrendered by the U.S. government under pressure and to avoid anarchy in the cities. Another tendency stresses self-determination by the black community but leaves loose just where this black community actually is, referring usually to the "almost mystical concept of a nation within a nation." Then there are those who insist that those cities and counties where blacks constitute 25 percent and upward of the population are the "black man's land" in the specifically American tradition of ethnic groups successively taking over power in the cities.

In addition to these tendencies, which at least begin to give Black Power a habitation, a name, and the perspective of rule or government over specific areas or political units, there are also those who think of Black Power purely in psychological terms—i.e., as black pride and black consciousness—and who see no possibility of blacks as a group ever achieving any rule. This tendency in turn can be divided into two: 1) Middle-class blacks for whom black pride and black consciousness are now fashionable and who think of this pride and consciousness as giving greater motivation to blacks to succeed in American life; and 2) black youth in whose heads black pride and black consciousness have exploded but who, without any perspective of blacks ever ruling, think only in terms of dying in the streets to prove their manhood. For these youth, now completely alienated from white society, aware that they have become expendable in terms of the labor process, despairing of any future, the only prospect is getting rid of as many whiteys as possible before whitey gets rid of them.

Fundamentally, the political perspective and objective around which the Black Power movement must now mobilize the masses and organize itself is the concept of Black Political Power in the cities and in those counties where blacks are a near or an actual majority. This perspective has both the urgency and legitimacy necessary to a successful struggle for power. The crisis in the cities is universally recognized as unresolvable by the existing power structure. Black Political Power has the legitimacy that comes from the concept of majority rule and from the specifically American tradition of successive ethnic groupings ruling in American cities. It has the additional legitimacy that comes from the fact that the whites have abandoned the cities to the blacks for the most flagrant racist reasons.

From the legitimacy of this perspective flows a very important fact in any power struggle, namely that the enemy (i.e., the white population which opposes Black Political Power) is put on the moral defensive. It then becomes clear that until white people in this country are ready to accept black power in the cities and in rural counties where blacks are a majority with the same flexibility as they accepted Irish and Italian power in the past, they are infected with racism. But the concept does not have moral power alone. The alternative to Black Political Power is not an inter-racial society, however much it is or is not desired. Such a society exists only in dreams. Nor is it realistic to think that blacks will eventually get tired of struggling and drift back into their "place." No, the only real alternative to Black Political Power in the sense demanded is unending crises in the cities, crime in the streets, long hot summers, naked military occupation and curfews, all of which not only affect the black community but also the white, creating a dangerous society, repressing civil liberties, crippling the economy, destroying any possibility of normal life. All these are no longer just threats. They are a reality which has already been experienced.

Thus the perspective of Black Political Power in the cities and rural areas confronts blacks and whites today with real alternatives in the same fundamental sense as the civil rights movement under King's leadership confronted blacks and whites with real alternatives. True, it was easier for whites in the South and North to accept desegregation in public accommodation than it is for them to accept Black Political Power. But it is also true that the alternative to Black Political Power is much more catastropic.

Based on this perspective, the Black Power movement can mobilize the masses through concrete struggles for facets of municipal and rural power: black control of schools to reverse the dangerously low achievement levels of black children, black control of the police to stop police brutality, black school superintendents or police commissioners and sheriffs, black mayors, black judges. The achievement of any of these not only whets the appetite of blacks for more, but creates the "white backlash" which is creative conflict in the sense that it forces the black movement to escalate sights to the conquest of power in order to defend its gains. In the course of these struggles, the movement is also forced to create the parallel hierarchies which are necessary for any new ruling group. It is also forced to explore what changes black rule will have to initiate in order to solve the problems of the cities in every sphere, including educa-

tion, social services, relations to regions, state and federal government, housing, health, etc.

As the definition and goals of Black Power become more concrete, so also does the definition of the role of whites. In the
period of Black Power as "black nationalism" or "black pride"
and "black consciousness," there was no necessity to think about
whites. Not only were they in the way physically, but just asking
blacks to think about their role seemed an imposition and a form
of white self-centeredness. However, as we move into the stage
of black revolutionary nationalism, or the serious struggle for
power, it is obvious that the revolutionary government can and
must use any forces which it has available to weaken, divide, or
immobilize the enemy. Up to now the black movement has not
addressed itself to this question primarily because it has not resolved the question of what it is concretely struggling for.

In the white community there are various tendencies, just as
there are in the black community. The overwhelming majority of
whites, of course, just wish that the black problem or blacks
themselves would disappear. But most whites now know that this
is impossible without a kind of genocidal offensive for which
white America is not ready. The power structure hopes that the
pouring of funds into the black community, in the form of anti-
poverty programs, swimming pools, etc., will contain or pacify
the blacks. If these do not succeed, then it is ready to resort to
military measures to maintain "law and order."

In one sense the average white worker or middle-class person
does not care how much the power structure does for the black
community. The rub, however, is that he feels the pinch in his
pocketbook in the form of taxes and therefore becomes increasingly susceptible to the agitation of the out-and-out fascist who
holds up before him the threat of blacks invading the white community, raping white women, etc. For these out-and-out fascists
Hitler's "final solution" is not unacceptable. Meanwhile, they lead
other whites toward that goal by their nightly meetings, their
gun drills, their insistence that the black movement is being led
by Communists, etc.

Finally, there is a very small percentage of whites who recognize that this society is bankrupt and look to the black revolution

as their only salvation, both for their own survival in the face of the world black revolution, and for the salvaging of old values and the creation of new ones. In the struggle for Black Political Power in the cities and in rural areas where blacks are a near or actual majority, these whites can play an important role. They can confront other whites with the legitimacy of Black Political Power, dividing and immobilizing their opposition to it. In the many areas where there are no blacks or only an infinitesimal number of blacks, they can confront other whites in a struggle for power over issues that are vital to them and thereby overcome the sympathizer's position of struggling only out of concern for blacks and not in terms of their own needs and their own survival. Only after revolutionary whites have taken some power from other whites now in power can they sit down with revolutionary blacks who have also wrested some power from some whites and as equals with power lay the basis for the future relationship of the new social forces in United States society.

*1968*

# 10
# Democracy: Capitalism's Last Battle-Cry

When *The American Revolution* was written in 1963, it was already apparent that certain myths and mystiques about the workers in the advanced capitalist countries had become obsolete. Also obsolete was the old colonialism in its naked form of political domination over colonial peoples; the order of the day had become neo-colonialism, which is a more subtle means of maintaining control over the material resources of Africa, Asia, and Latin America.

Since that time the war in Vietnam has exposed the determination of the United States to act as the policeman of the world by whatever means necessary, and to be the counter-revolutionary center opposed to the revolutionary determination of the people of Africa, Asia, and Latin America to control their own destinies. Since that time also the black rebellion inside the United States has revealed that the status of blacks in this country is essentially that of a colonized people systematically kept in that status by every sector of the population.

In my original introduction I stated that "I believe in democracy but I don't believe in being too damn democratic." I went on to say that

> I believe that everyone has a right to his opinion, but I don't believe he has a right to be hypocritical or sly about it, and I believe that it is my responsibility to fight and right those opinions that are wrong. . . . A baby is not born with hate, but a lot of babies in the United States are taught hate. Those who have the most power can do the most shaping and the most teaching, and if they are teaching what I believe is wrong, then I believe their power should be taken away from them.

122

It was clear to me then, and it becomes clearer to me every day, that there are too many myths and prejudices about the inherent value of democracy itself. The United States has been a democracy for over 150 years, yet no one has dared to question whether a system which has existed under uniquely favorable conditions for so long and has kept a whole race in subjugation is itself worth maintaining. Historically, democracy is and always has been a means whereby a few could have certain rights at the expense of the many. The Greeks invented democracy but never freed the slaves. The capitalist societies adopted democracy but never freed black people in the colonies either outside their borders or, as in the United States, inside them.

While white United States citizens have been breathing the same air, inhabiting the same land, talking about dictatorship and fascism in other countries, and boasting about their democracy at home, black people have been living under fascism right beside them. Now that blacks, who over the years have been called everything but citizen (boy, girl, uncle, aunt, our colored people, etc.), have revolted, allegedly in order to achieve democracy for themselves, whatever emerges from this revolt cannot possibly be the same system which has been operating all these years as American democracy.

If the black revolt does not succeed—which is possible—then Americans are going to discover what it is like to live as the black man has been living all these years, in constant terror of violence from the mob and from the police, never certain what rights he can exercise under the law and under the Constitution, always wondering which ones among his so-called protectors in the police force and in the courts still retain a vestige of human decency and which ones are in league with the mob to put him away or wipe him out.

In fact, such a reign of terror has already begun for white Americans, as evidenced by the political assassinations of whites during the last few years: two at "Ole Miss" in September 1962, William Moore in Alabama, John F. Kennedy and his alleged slayer in Texas in 1963, Goodman and Schwerner in Mississippi in 1964, Robert F. Kennedy in Los Angeles in 1968. During this same period, along with the genocide in Vietnam, there have been countless political assassinations of blacks, among them the four little girls in an Alabama church, Medgar Evers, Colonel Lemuel Penn, James Chaney, Malcolm X, Martin Luther King, Vernon Dahmer in Mississippi, Bobby Hutton in Oakland, California, the three youths at the Algiers Motel in Detroit, and hundreds of others in Watts, Newark, Detroit, Washington, D.C., and practically every other American city.

These murders are only the most dramatic signs of the new brute realities. Everywhere in the country, in the North and in the South, white Americans are beginning to discover that the democracy of which they have been so proud has been a myth that could only survive as long as it was not seriously tested. In the North, in particular, liberal whites are beginning to experience the isolation and fears that Southern liberals have known for years as all around them, every night and in every block, they realize that their neighbors are meeting and conspiring, formally and informally, to counter the black revolution; that they are checking off the names of those in the neighborhood and in public office who can be counted on and those who must be immobilized or eliminated when the showdown comes; assigning individuals to write "hate" letters, make "hate" phone calls, and contact officials in key positions; organizing cells inside the police force, the National Guard, and the armed services; buying and selling the innumerable varieties of "hate" literature that are now available; posting warnings at the borders of white communities warning blacks to "keep out"; building arsenals and training Minutemen to invade black areas. In every Northern community today there is at least one white liberal who is beginning to feel as alone and as apprehensive as the black who drives up to a service station in the South.

Many people will admit that this is what is now taking place, but most of them will deny that this is American democracy. American democracy, they insist, is what they believe in or what they can make by their faith and their deeds. But after a system has existed for this long, it has to be judged by what it is and what it has been, not by the alleged hopes or faiths of its founders or supporters. And what American democracy is today is only the coming to the surface, the appearance, of what its underlying essence has been all along. The difference is that now, for the first time, it can be seen clearly to be what in truth it always has been.

The truth is that the democracy of which Americans have been so proud is based on the worst kind of class system in the world, a class system that is based on the systematic exploitation of another race. Racism is the philosophy which pursues or condones the systematic oppression of another race because that race is inferior or subhuman. If the American people had not been racist, they could never have boasted about American democracy all these years.

American democracy is unlike other democracies the world has known. Under the Western democracies (including American democracy) there has been more systematic exploitation of more people than there has ever been under any other political system. (He who doubts this need only look at a world map.) Other Western democracies super-exploited the people abroad in order to accelerate progress in the motherland; the colonial people were the underclass. In the United States, on the other hand, the under-class that has been systematically super-exploited in order to make progress possible for the dominant race has lived in the same country and therefore its systematic oppression has had to be systematically justified by a philosophy of racial supremacy. In other advanced countries although the ordinary working people lived better than the super-exploited people of the colonies, for the most part they remained in the working class. In the United States, however, because there was a race of black men, women, and children kept at the bottom by force, by habit, and by ideology, other workers could climb up on their backs into the middle class and feel that in so doing they were living up to the highest ideals of American democracy.

Thus, American democracy has become, in fact, a way of life whose most cherished value is climbing up on the backs of others to get to the top. This is what the American "classless society" is—using others, and particularly those of other races, to advance yourself materially and socially, without regard to right and wrong and without regard to social responsibility. What has been boasted about as the "opportunity" to rise above your class in

America has been, in reality, opportunism. What has been boasted about as the "freedom of the individual" has been, in reality, the freedom to purchase material goods regardless of human values. What has been boasted about as "government of the people" has been, in reality, the evasion by the people of the social responsibilities of self-government.

These are the truths underlying the myth of American democracy which are coming to light as a result of the black revolution, a revolution which is still in its very early stages.

Until now it has not been easy for Americans to accept that there might be any system better than democracy. The only alternatives they have been able to envisage are those which they have seen operating in other countries, socialism, communism, and fascism. They have condemned all three but have actually felt a close kinship with the last because it corresponds so closely to their actual practices against black people at home and abroad. Actually, the kind of new society that will be created as the revolution advances in this country is dependent upon the specific conditions in this country at this time, just as American democracy itself developed out of the specific conditions in this country at another time. One of the most important of these specific conditions is the material abundance which means there is enough for each to have according to his needs.

One thing is certain. Now that the black bottom of American society is in unheaval, it is not only the place of everybody on the upper rungs of the ladder which is in jeopardy. The very system of climbing up on the backs of others to get to the top is threatened. For this reason, the black revolution, coming at this time in America, opens up the possibility of a real classless society rather than the "classless society" which has in fact rested on the class subjugation of another race.

Up to now most radicals and Marxists have refused to face the fact that the successful revolutions of this century have taken place in underdeveloped countries and that there has not been a successful revolution in a highly advanced capitalist country. Nor have they consciously sought to advance Marx's analysis beyond 1848 by a systematic stage-by-stage analysis of what has been happening to the two sides of capitalism, capital and labor.

Instead they have continued to talk about the working class as the social force of world revolution. Meanwhile, capitalism has been able to utilize its two tentacles, colonialism and neo-colonialism, to advance itself and to incorporate the workers in the advanced countries into the capitalist system itself, not only through higher wages, job security, pensions, compensation, Medicare, life insurance, etc., but by giving them a sense of being racially superior (i.e., of being more culturally advanced) to the people of the colonial world within and without. The more the Marxists make excuses for these workers, the more racist they themselves sound to the racially oppressed peoples. For it is obvious that in their support of colonialism, neo-colonialism and the counter-revolutionary wars of the American warfare state, United States workers differ from United States capitalists only in their greater crudity. There is no question in my mind that if Marx himself were around today, his scientific methodology would have long since enabled him to recognize the industrial workers' incorporation into the highly advanced capitalist system. But Marx is dead, so the fault lies with those who continue to call themselves Marxists but who have not continued the scientific—i.e., historical—method of analysis which Marx initiated.

In the four-fifths of the world which has been systematically damned to underdevelopment by colonialism and neo-colonialism, it is not difficult to define and mobilize the revolutionary social forces in a struggle for political independence. The chief problem, once political independence has been achieved, is how to combine the satisfaction of the masses' overwhelming immediate needs with the accumulation and development of the productive forces that are essential for continuing development. In the industrialized nations, on the other hand, the chief difficulty is, first, to define which *are* the revolutionary social forces and which are *not* the revolutionary social forces, and, second, to find how to develop the conflict between the revolutionary social forces and the existing power structure to the point of no return —to the point where they are totally irreconcilable as to means and ends.

Blacks in the United States constitute the only revolutionary social force at this stage both because they have been systematically damned to underdevelopment inside this economically most advanced and politically most backward society, and because, having been made expendable by technological advances, their very survival depends on their creating a new society in which politics rather than labor will be the socially necessary activity giving the system its rationale and order. This means that the black revolution must create a kind of society which goes far beyond any that have been achieved by the revolutions of the past.

In a capitalist society such as the United States, one which has been a warfare state for a whole generation, technological breakthroughs, financed by government grants and therefore through general taxation of the citizenry rather than through private capital, have become routine. The result is that automation and cybernation already make it technologically possible to free the overwhelming majority of the labor force from manual labor. The chief reason why the capitalists themselves have not taken advantage of this possibility is not the cost, which could be written off through tax deductions. It is that the system cannot solve the problem of how to discipline the human forces that would be released by the exploitation of machines rather than of men. Full employment is important to capitalism as a political weapon to discipline people—i.e., for pacification—even if full employment is no longer *economically* necessary. Hence the readiness, ever since the 1967 Detroit rebellion, of American Big Business, led by Henry Ford, to provide jobs for the "hard-core unemployed," the black outsiders who constitute such a menace to the system. Even Russia, whose agricultural problems remain unresolved but whose industrial sector has developed to the point of cybernation, is still so dependent upon the Protestant ethic (income in proportion to work) for its orderly functioning that new machinery which will release large numbers of workers is not introduced until careful surveys have been made as to where this manpower can be relocated.

Once the revolutionary social force and the historical objectives of the revolution have been determined, the question of where and how to mobilize this force for revolution must still be evaluated scientifically. In the United States the city is the terrain of the struggle. Millions of blacks have been forced into the large industrial and transportation centers by the mechanization of agriculture, in one of the greatest mass migrations of modern times. Concentrated in the cities but no longer needed to man the industrial plants, these people constitute a continuous and growing threat to the power structure which, lacking the economic means to discipline them, is driven to ever more rigorous and vicious police-state measures. For their own survival, therefore, blacks must control these cities politically, socially, and economically.

The big American city, with its concentration of economic, political, and social resources, is today the black man's land. The cities have become to today's revolutionary social force what the factories were to the workers in the 1930's.

The simultaneous rebellion of the black masses in major cities would create a mass disruption of production, transportation, communications, and all political and social institutions greater than that created by the strikes of the 1930's and comparable to that created by the recent general strike in France. This would be the effect of spontaneous rebellion. On a planned scale it could result in the complete control of the cities, and therefore of the heart of the nation.

Ever since the spring of 1963, when the conflict between the police and the blacks of Birmingham, Alabama, moved the struggle into the cities, the black revolution has become an increasing challenge to the system and all those, including the white workers, who support the system. The question is no longer one of rights but of power. Who will control City Hall? The police? The schools? The stores, banks, and factories inside the black man's land? The mass communications media? Those who are presently in power or those who are presently powerless, the whites or the blacks? Just as the first civil war in the United States was a war to determine whether the North or the South would control the Western territories, today's civil war is to determine who will control the very real and substantial resources of the cities.

It is this very real war between blacks and whites for very

real power which has caused such consternation among old radicals and among liberals. Even though they admit the completely counter-revolutionary, corrupt, and bankrupt character of American (white power) institutions, these whites cannot accept the idea of a revolution led by blacks and a new power instituted by blacks that will completely revolutionize this country from bottom to top and from top to bottom. That is why so many of them continue to be for integration, even though it is obvious that integration means class collaboration, pacification, and incorporation into the system. That is the reason for their efforts to scare blacks away from a revolutionary struggle for Black Power by emphasizing the minority position of blacks on an overall national scale instead of the majority position of blacks in the key cities. Blacks usually reply to this point by emphasizing their close ties to the world revolution of the people of Asia, Africa, and Latin America, who constitute four-fifths of the world population.

However, scientifically speaking blacks need not be on the political defensive just because they are a minority. All revolutions are started by a minority. The majority usually vacillates back and forth and from side to side, waiting and watching to see which side will win, sometimes participating with the revolutionary forces and sometimes with the counter-revolutionary forces, and finally ending up on the side of the victors.

The revolutionary struggle in the United States is a struggle between Black Power and White Power in which the blacks are a very substantial minority. At the same time, it would be a mistake to regard all whites as completely homogeneous and frozen in their positions with regard to the revolution. Splits and conflicts among whites can be and should be sharpened. At the present time the only section of the white population which shows any sign of being a potentially revolutionary social force is the university students. Brought into the struggle by the blacks, the students joined the civil rights movement with the paternalistic idea that they were helping blacks to win democratic rights and thus reform American society. After they were forced out of the movement when it entered the Black Power stage, these students were at first demoralized; they then began to confront the issues of their own survival in relation to the Vietnam war and the industrial and military establishment. They began to recognize that they too have enemies and that all too often these enemies are not only white, but are their own parents.

These students are a growing potential revolutionary force with a strategically important relationship to a highly technical productive apparatus which needs the intellectual worker much more than it needs the manual worker. Their own survival as potential draftees requires their opposition to America's counter-revolutionary wars against the world revolution. Because of their own experiences with the old working class which supports these wars, they do not mouth the "black and white, unite and fight" slogans of the old radicals. Whether and to what extent they will actually become allies of the black revolution depends upon the dynamics of the struggle. The leadership of the American Revolution can only come from the blacks. This is, first of all, because blacks are the only ones who, as a mass, cannot be incorporated into the system; and secondly, since they have been systematically excluded from Western civilization and culture for so many generations, they are not prisoners of Western methods of thought. They are therefore the ones best able to do what the Asian revolution has done, exploit the weaknesses of Western strategy, which is ultimately based on Western methods of thought, to defeat the counter-revolution.

A revolution is not just a transfer of power but a war on the part of the powerless to take power by all means necessary. It is only in the course of such a war that the revolutionary social forces develop with the necessary clarity their ultimate objectives, the parallel structures and the leadership necessary to achieve them, the consciousness that what they are fighting for is not only right but theirs by right, and the aggressiveness and historical confidence that are necessary for victory. It takes two to make a revolution—the revolution and the counter-revolution—and the revolution must create a long-range strategy for its own victory and the defeat of the enemy.

The black movement is presently engaged in the very difficult process of creating such a strategy. The task will not be completed in a day, a month, a year, or in the course of a hot summer. The first soviets were formed in Russia in 1905, but the Russian Revolution did not succeed until 1917. The Chinese Revolution took over twenty years. The African revolution, which began with the political independence of Ghana in 1957, is only now beginning to assume the form of the continental armed struggle against colonialism and neo-colonialism essential to Pan-African unity and therefore to African independence.

The most urgent task for the American Revolution today is the creation of the long-range strategy by the black revolutionary movement. The shape of the revolution has already become crystallized. It is a war whose chief terrain will be the big cities and whose goal is the total liberation and the total reorganization of society. In this war each individual will be judged: Is he with the revolution or is he with the counter-revolution? Now the task is to do what Sun Tzu advised over two thousand years ago in the *Art of War:* "Shape" the enemy, size up his strengths and weaknesses and develop strategy and tactics to suit.

*1968*

# 11

# The Myth
# and Irrationality
# of Black Capitalism

I cannot account for why many of us are here, but the fact that we *are* here indicates to me that the black movement has now reached the stage where it compels us to confront the question: What kind of economic system do black people need at this stage in history? What kind of economic system do we envisage, not as a question for abstract discussion, but as the foundation on which we can mobilize the black masses to struggle, understanding that their future is at stake?

It is now nearly fifteen years since the black movement started out to achieve civil rights through integration into the system. Year after year the movement has gained momentum until today millions of black people in all strata of life consider themselves part of the movement. At no other time in our 400 years on this continent have black people sustained such a long period of activity. We have had rebellions and revolts of short duration, but it is quite apparent that what we are now engaged in is not just a revolt, not just a rebellion, but a full-fledged movement driving toward full growth and maturity and therefore requiring a serious examination of the fundamental nature of the system that we are attacking and the system that we are trying to build.

It is also now quite clear that black people, who have been the chief victims of the system that is under attack, are the ones who have to make this examination; because for us it is a very concrete and not just an abstract question. We have evaded this question because in reality we recognized that to tamper with the system is to tamper with the whole society and all its institutions.

Now we cannot evade the question any longer.

When we talk about the system, we are talking about capitalism. I repeat: When we talk about the system, we are talking about capitalism. Let us not be afraid to say it. And when we talk about capitalism, we are talking about the system that has created the situation that blacks are in today! Let us be clear about that too. Black underdevelopment is a product of capitalist development. Black America is underdeveloped today because of capitalist semi-colonialism, just as Africa, Asia, and Latin America are underdeveloped today because of capitalist colonialism. We cannot look at the underdevelopment of the black community separately from capitalism any more than we can look at the development of racism separately from capitalism.

The illusion that we could resolve racism without talking about the economic system came to an end when we arrived at the point of talking about power to control and develop our communities. Now we are forced to face the question of what system to reject and what system to adopt. This has forced us to face squarely the relationship of racism to capitalism.

Capitalism in the United States is unique because, unlike capitalism elsewhere—which first exploited its indigenous people and then fanned out through colonialism to exploit other races in other countries—it started out by dispossessing one set of people (the Indians) and then importing another set of people (the Africans) to do the work on the land. This method of enslavement not only made blacks the first working class in the country to be exploited for their *labor* but made blacks the foundation of the capital necessary for early industrialization.

As I pointed out in the *Manifesto for a Black Revolutionary Party:**

> Black people were not immigrants to this country but captives, brought here for the purpose of developing the economy of British America. The traffic in slaves across the Atlantic stimulated Northern shipping. The slave and sugar trade in the West Indies nourished Northern distilleries. Cotton grown on Southern plantations vitalized Northern textile industries. So slavery was not only indispensable to the Southern economy; it was indispensable to the *entire* national economy.

---

* Philadelphia: Pacesetters Publishing House, 1969.

At the same time the land on which American Southern plantations and Northern farms were developed was taken from the Indians. Thus Indian dispossession and African slavery are the twin foundations of white economic advancement in North America. No section of the country was not party to the defrauding of the red man or the enslavement of the Black.

What white people had achieved by force and for the purpose of economic exploitation in the beginning, they then sanctified by ideology. People of color, they rationalized, are by nature inferior; therefore, *every* person of color should be subordinated to *every* white person in *every* sphere, even where economic profit is not involved. The economic exploitation of man required by capitalism, wheresoever situated, having assumed in this country the historical form of the economic exploitation of the Black and red man, this historical form was now given the authority of an eternal truth. Racism acquired a dynamic of its own, and armed with this ideology white Americans from all strata of life proceeded to structure *all* their institutions for the systematic subordination and oppression of Blacks. . . .

The early struggles to abolish the relatively superficial manifestations of racism in public accommodations have now developed into struggles challenging the racism structured into *every* American institution and posing the need to reorganize these institutions from their very foundations. Housing, factories, schools and universities; labor unions, churches, prisons and the armed services; sports, entertainment, the mass media and fraternal organizations; health, welfare, hospitals and cemeteries; domestic and foreign politics and government at all levels; industry, transportation and communications; the professions, the police and the courts; organized and unorganized crime; even a partial listing of the institutions now being challenged suggests the magnitude of the social revolution that is involved.

In the course of its escalating struggles, the Black movement has steadily and irreversibly deprived all these institutions of their legitimacy and their supposed immunity.

I said earlier that black underdevelopment is the result of capitalist development. At the bottom of every ladder in American society is a black man. His place there is a direct result of capitalism supporting racism and racism supporting capitalism. Today, in an effort to protect this capitalist system, the white power structure is seeking once again to re-enslave black people by offering them black capitalism. Now, scientifically speaking, there is no such thing as a black capitalism which is different from white capitalism or capitalism of any other color. Capitalism, regardless of its color, is a system of exploitation of one set of people by another set of people. The very laws of capitalism require that some forces have to be exploited.

This effort on the part of the power structure has already caused certain members of the black race, including some who have been active in the movement, to believe that self-determination can be achieved by coexistence with capitalism—that is, integration into the system. In reality, black capitalism is a dream and a delusion. Blacks have no one underneath them to exploit. So black capitalism would have to exploit a black labor force which is already at the bottom of the ladder and is in no mood to change from one exploiter to another just because he is of the same color.

Nevertheless, as residents and indigenous members of the black community we recognize its need for development. Our question, therefore, is how *can* it be developed? How *should* it be developed? To answer these questions, we must clarify the nature of its underdevelopment.

The physical structure and environment of the black community is underdeveloped not because it has never been at a stage of high industrial development but because it has been devastated by the wear and tear of constant use in the course of the industrial development of this country. Scientifically speaking, the physical undevelopment of the black community is decay. Black communities are used communities, the end result and the aftermath of rapid economic development. The undevelopment of black communities, like that of the colonies in Africa, Asia, and Latin America, is a product of capitalist development. At the same time there is an important difference between the economic undevelopment of a colony in Africa, Asia, or Latin America, and the economic undevelopment of the black community inside an advanced country like the United States.

The economic undevelopment of a colony is the result of the fact that the colony's natural and historical process of development was interrupted and destroyed by colonialism, so that large sections of the country have been forced to become or remain pre-industrial or agricultural. For example, many of these societies once had their own handicraft industries which were destroyed by Western economic penetration. Most were turned into one-crop countries to supply raw materials or agricultural produce to the Western imperialists. In struggling for independence from imperialism, these societies are fighting for the opportunity to develop themselves industrially.

On the other hand, the physical structure of the black communities inside the United States is the direct result of industrial development, which has turned these communities into wastelands, abandoned by an industry that has undergone technological revolutions. The physical structure of black communities is like that of the abandoned mining communities in Appalachia whose original reason for existence has been destroyed by the discovery of new forms of energy or whose coal veins were exhausted by decades of mining. It would be sheer folly and naiveté to propose reopening these mines and starting the process of getting energy from their coal all over again. When one form of production has been rendered obsolete and a community devastated by an earlier form of capitalist exploitation, it would be supporting a superstition to propose its rehabilitation by a repetition of the past. You don't hear any proposals for white capitalism in Appalachia, do you?

Secondly, the black community is not technologically backward in the same way as the majority of communities in an undeveloped nation in Asia, Africa, or Latin America are. In these countries the vast majority of people still live on the land and, until recently, had had experience in using only the most elementary agricultural tools, such as the hoe or the plough. In these countries a revolution in agriculture must accompany the industrial revolution. By contrast, the mechanization of agriculture has already taken place in the United States, forcing the black people (who were this country's first working class on the land) to move to the cities. The great majority of blacks have now lived in the city for the last generation and have been exposed to the most modern appliances and machinery. In the use or production of these appliances and machines, the blacks are no less developed than the great majority of white workers.

The undevelopment of blacks is primarily in two areas:

1. They have been systematically excluded from the supervisory, planning, and decision-making roles which would have given them practical experience and skills in organizing, planning, and administration.

2. They have been systematically excluded from the higher education which would have given them the abstract and conceptual tools necessary for research and technological innovation at *this* stage of economic development, when productivity is more dependent on imagination, knowledge, and the concepts of systems—on mental processes—than it is on manual labor.

From the preceding analysis we can propose certain fundamental guidelines for any programs aimed at developing black communities:

1. Black communities are today capitalist communities, communities which have been developed by capitalist methods. Their present stage of decay, decline, and dilapidation—their present stage of undevelopment—is a product of capitalist exploitation. They have been used and re-used to produce profit by every form of capitalist: landlords, construction industries, merchants, insurance brokers, bankers, finance companies, racketeers, and manufacturers of cars, appliances, steel, and every other kind of industrial commodity. Development for the black community means getting rid of these exploiters, *not* replacing white exploiters by black ones.

2. Any future development of the black community must start from the bottom up, not from the top down. The people at the very bottom of the black community, the chief victims of capitalist exploitation, cannot be delivered from their bottom position by black capitalist exploitation. They are the ones in the most pressing need of rapid development. They are also the fastest growing section of the black community. They are the black street force, the ADC mothers, welfare recipients, domestic servants, unskilled laborers, etc. These—not the relatively small black

middle class—are the people who must be given an opportunity to exercise initiative, to make important decisions, and to get a higher education, if the black community is to be developed. The creation of a middle class of black capitalists would make the distribution of income inside the black community less equal, not more equal. It would be the source of greater chaos and dis- order inside the black community, not more order and stability, because the layer at the bottom of the black community, far from seeing these black capitalists as models and symbols to be admired and imitated, would be hostile to and strike out at them.

3. Struggle should be built into any program of black com- munity development in order to stimulate crisis learning and escalate and expand the sense of civic rights and responsibilities. The struggles should be on issues related to the concrete griev- ances most deeply felt by the lowest layer of the black community —on issues of education, welfare, health, housing, police brutal- ity—and should be aimed at mobilizing this layer for control of these institutions inside the black community as the only means to reverse the manifest failure of these institutions to meet the needs of black people. It is only through struggle over such griev- ances that the largest and most important section of the black community can be involved in decision-making. The most im- portant obstacle to the development of the black community is the lack of power on the part of blacks, and particularly on the part of this section of the black community, and therefore the lack of conviction that anything they do can be meaningful. It is only through struggles for control of these institutions that they can achieve a degree of power and an increasing awareness of their importance and their responsibilities. Only through struggle can a community be developed out of individuals and the leader- ship necessary to any community be created.

4. Any program for the development of the black community must provide for and encourage development at an extremely rapid, crash program, pace and not at an evolutionary or gradual pace. Otherwise, in view of the rapid growth of the black popu- lation, and particularly of its most oppressed sector, deterioration will proceed more rapidly than development. For example, in a

community where there is a pressing need for at least 10,000 low-cost housing units, the building of a couple of hundred units here and there in the course of a year does not begin to fill the need for the original 10,000 units—while at the same time another thousand or more units have deteriorated far below livable level. The same principle applies to medical and health care. To set up a program for a few hundred addicts a year is ridiculous when there are hundreds of new addicts being created every week.

5. The black community cannot possibly be developed by introducing into it the trivial skills and the outmoded technology of yesteryear. Proposals for funding small businesses which can only use sweatshop methods or machinery which is already or will soon become obsolete means funding businesses which are bound to fail, thereby increasing the decay in the black community. Proposals for vocational training or employment of the hard-core in black or white businesses (on the theory that what black people need most to develop the black community is the discipline of work and money in their pockets) are simply proposals for pacification and for maintaining the black community in its present stage of undevelopment. There is absolutely no point in training blacks for dead-end jobs such as assembly work, clerical bank work, court reporting, elevator operating, drafting, clerking, meter reading, mail clerking, oil field or packing house working, painting, railroad maintenance, service station attending, steel mill or textile working. There is little point in training blacks for status quo jobs, such as accountant, auto mechanic, bank teller, bricklayer, truck driver, TV and appliance repairing, sheet metal worker. There is great demand for these jobs now, but new methods and new processes will make these jobs obsolete within the next decade. The jobs for which blacks should be educated are the jobs of the future, such as aerospace engineers, recreation directors, dentists, computer programmers, mass media production workers, communications equipment experts, medical technicians, operations researchers, teachers, quality control. There can be no economic development of the black community unless black people are developed for these jobs with a bright future.

At the same time the preparation of blacks for these bright future jobs must not be confined to simply giving them skills. In the modern world, productivity depends upon continued innovation which in turn depends upon research and the overall concepts needed for consciously organized change. The only practical education for black people, therefore, is an education which increases their eagerness to learn by giving them not only a knowledge of what is known but challenges them to explore what is still unknown, and to interpret, project, and imagine. The only practical enterprises to develop the black community are those which are not only producing for today but which include research and development and the continuing education of their employees as an integral part of their present ongoing program.

Black youth, born during the space age, are particularly aware not only of the racism which has always confined blacks to dead-end jobs but of the revolutionary changes which are a routine part of modern industry. Any attempt to interest them in dead-end jobs or in education for dead-end jobs will only increase the decay and disorder in the black community, because rather than accept these jobs or this education, black youth will take to the streets. Any programs for developing the black community must have built into them the greatest challenge to the imagination, ingenuity, and potential of black youth. What youth, and particularly black youth, find hard to do are the "little things." What can mobilize their energies is "the impossible."

6. Any program for the development of the black community must be based on large-scale social ownership rather than on private individual enterprise. In this period of large-scale production and distribution, private individual enterprises (or small businesses) can only remain marginal and dependent, adding to the sense of hopelessness and powerlessness inside the black community.

The social needs of the community, consciously determined by the community, *not* the needs or interests of particular individual entrepreneurs, must be the determining fact in the allocation of resources. The philosophy that automatic progress will result for the community if enterprising individuals are allowed to pursue their private interests must be consciously rejected. Equally illusory is the idea that development of the black community can take place through the operation of "blind" or "unseen" economic forces. The black community can only be developed through community control of the public institutions, public funds, and other community resources, including land inside the black community, all of which are in fact the public property of the black community.

Massive educational programs, including programs of struggle, must be instituted inside the black community to establish clearly in the minds of black people the fact that the institutions which most directly affect the lives of the deepest layer of the black community (schools, hospitals, law-enforcement agencies, welfare agencies) are the property of the black community, paid for by our taxes, and that therefore the black community has the right to control the funds which go into the operation and administration of these institutions. This right is reinforced and made more urgent by the fact that these institutions have completely failed to meet black needs while under white control.

All over the country today the police are organizing themselves into independent *political* organizations, outside the control of elected civilian officials and challenging the right of civilian administrations and the public, whom they are allegedly employed to protect, to control them. Community control of the police is no longer just a slogan or an abstract concept. It is a concrete necessity in order to overcome the increasing danger of lawlessness and disorder that is inherent in the swelling movement toward independent bodies of armed men wearing the badges of law and order but acting as a rallying point for militant white extremists.

In these campaigns special emphasis should also be placed on the question of land reform and acquisition. Over the last thirty years, the federal government has changed land tenure and agricultural technology through massive subsidies involving the plowing-under of vast areas of land, rural electrification, agricultural research, etc. But all this has been for the benefit of whites who have become millionaire farmers and landowners, at the expense of blacks who have been driven off the land altogether or have been retained as farm laborers, averaging less than $5.00 a day, or $800 a year, in wages.

In the South the black community must undertake a massive land reform movement to force the federal government to turn these plowed-under lands over to the millions of blacks still in the South, for black community organizations to develop. Black community development of these areas in the South should include not only the organization of producers' and distributors' cooperatives but also the organization of agricultural research institutes, funded by the federal government, where blacks working on the land can combine production and management with continuing education, research, and innovation. The responsibility of government for funding research in relation to agricultural development is well established. Nobody has a greater right to these funds than the blacks now in the South and other blacks who will be drawn back to the South to assist in community development of agricultural lands.

In order that the black people in these agricultural areas do not fall behind their brothers and sisters in the cities, land in these communities should also be set aside for recreation, medical facilities, and for operation of advanced communication centers.

A similar campaign for land reform and acquisition should be organized in the urban areas of the North where the great majority of blacks are now concentrated. The concept of "eminent domain," or the acquisition of private property for public use, has already been well established in the Urban Renewal program. However, up to now "eminent domain" has been exercised only in the interest of white developers and residents, and against the interests of black homeowners and the black community. Federal subsidies have been used to expel blacks from their homes, businesses, and churches, and then to improve the areas which have then been turned over to private developers to build homes for middle-class and wealthy whites.

The principle of "eminent domain" must now be employed to acquire land for the purposes of the black community. Vacant land, land owned by whites which has been allowed to deteriorate, etc., must be acquired and turned over to black communities to plan and develop under black control and with black labor, for the purpose of creating communities which will meet the many-sided needs of black people for housing, health, education, recreation, shopping facilities, etc., and which will be a source of participation, pride, and inspiration to the black community and particularly to black youth.

The black community cannot be developed unless black youth, in particular, are given real and not just rhetorical opportunities to participate in the actual planning and development of the black community. The feeling which black youth have now is that the *streets* of the black community belong to them. But without a positive and concrete program to involve them in the planning and construction of the black community, they can only wander these streets angrily and aimlessly, each one a potential victim of white-controlled dope rings.

The application of the concept of social ownership and control by the black community is essential to the involvement of the black street force in the development of the black community. These "untouchables" have no property which they can call their own and absolutely no reason to believe that they will ever acquire any. The only future before them is in the prisons, the military, or the streets. They are the ones who have sparked the urban rebellions. Yet, up to now, after each rebellion they have been excluded from participation, while middle-class blacks have presumed to speak for them and to extract petty concessions which have uplifted these blacks but have left the "untouchables" out in the cold. The "untouchables" have not been organized into decision-making bodies with issues and grievances and aspirations and rights to development. Instead, middle-class blacks have been used to pacify them. But the fact is that these street forces will not just disappear. They are growing by leaps and bounds, threatening not only the system but also those who stand between them and the system, including those blacks who presume to speak for them.

7. Since pacification of these rebellious forces has been the chief purpose of all so-called development programs, it is no accident that most of these programs have been single-action, one-year, or "one hot summer" programs, without any funda-

mental perspective for developing new social institutions or for resolving the basic issues and grievances which affect the largest section of the black community.

On the other hand, it is obvious that any serious programs for the development of the black community must be based on comprehensive planning for at least a five-year period. Piecemeal, single-action, one-year, or "one hot summer" programs are worse than no programs at all. They constitute tokenism in the economic sphere and produce the same result as tokenism in any sphere: the increased discontent of the masses of the community.

The purpose of these five-year comprehensive programs must be the reconstruction and reorganization of all the social institutions inside the black community which have manifestly failed to meet the needs of the black community. Any programs for the development of the black community which are worth funding at all must be programs that are not just for the curing of defects. Rather they must be for the purpose of creating new types of social institutions through the mobilization of the social creativity of black youth, ADC mothers, welfare recipients, and all those in the black community who are the main victims of the systematic degradation and exploitation of American racism. Development for the black community at this stage in history means *social ownership, social change, social pioneering,* and *social reconstruction.*

*1969*

# 12

# Uprooting
# Racism and Racists
# in the United States

In March 1968, one month before the racist murder of Dr. Martin
Luther King Jr., the President's Commission on Civil Disorders,
headed by Illinois Governor Otto Kerner, issued its monumental
report charging white racism with responsibility for the degraded
conditions of blacks in this country. In the year and a half since
the report appeared, white racist hostility toward blacks, particularly among white workers, has increased, not decreased. Polls
indicate that today fewer whites believe that blacks are the
victims of discrimination, and that, in fact, a growing number
of whites believe that blacks are the villains rather than the
victims.

The obvious contradiction of the Kerner report is that after
diagnosing whites as responsible for racist oppression of blacks,
the report goes on to make recommendations for the treatment
not of *whites* but of blacks. As we pointed out at the time, "It is
like saying that the way to keep white sheriffs, policemen, Ku
Klux Klansmen, White Citizens' Councilmen, Minutemen, Birchites, and other American fascists from lynching any more blacks
is to put the blacks to work, send them to school, and build some
new housing developments in the ghetto." The victims are the
ones who need rehabilitation, the villains are not even ackowl-
edged to exist.

It is, of course, no accident that the Kerner Commission did
not tackle the question of white racists. First of all, the "white,
moderate, responsible, Establishment" Americans (in Tom

---

* This paper was written with Grace Lee Boggs.

Wicker's words\*) who made up the Commission are not in the habit of using their power to expose or confront the crimes and barbarism of white racists any more than the white, moderate, responsible Germans of Hitler's days were in the habit of exposing or confronting the crimes and barbarism of German racists. Note, for example, how little appears in the "white, moderate, responsible" American press today about Minutemen, KKKsmen, and Birchites, contrasted to the constant scare headlines about Black Panthers and other black militants.

Moreover, the Kerner Commission, including as it did such pillars of capitalism as the senior officials of North American Rockwell Corp., Litton Industries, General Mills Corp., Bank of America, etc., could hardly have been expected to undertake the kind of probe of white racism which might have led to its roots in capitalist economics and ideology. So from the outset the Commission made it clear that its aim was to attack "the root causes of racial disorder," not the root causes of racism.

It seems a minor difference, but those planning a career in journalism should pay it special attention. The one line of attack —against the root causes of racism—leads ultimately, as we shall show, to a revolution against the system. The other—against the root causes of racial disorder—leaves the door wide open for a counter-revolution against those making a revolution against the system. For it should be obvious to anyone not blinded by racism that the root cause of racial disorders in Northern cities over the last five years is the revolt against racism. If blacks were ready to submit to racism, there would be no racial disorders.

The first thing we have to understand is that racism is not a "mental quirk" or a "psychological flaw" on an individual's part.\*\* Racism is the systematized oppression by one race of another. In other words, the various forms of oppression within every sphere of social relations—economic exploitation, military subjugation, political subordination, cultural devaluation, psychological violation, sexual degradation, verbal abuse, etc.—together make up a

---

\* Special *Introduction* to the Kerner report.

\*\* See Frantz Fanon, "Racism and Culture," in *Toward the African Revolution* (New York and London: Monthly Review Press, 1967).

whole of interacting and developing processes which operate so normally and naturally and are so much a part of the existing institutions of the society that the individuals involved are barely conscious of their operation. As Fanon says, "The racist in a culture with racism is therefore normal."

This kind of systematic oppression of one race by another was unknown to mankind in the thousands of years of recorded history before the emergence of capitalism four hundred years ago—although racial prejudice was not unknown. For example, some Chinese in the third century B.C. considered yellow-haired, green-eyed people in a distant province barbarians. In Ancient Egypt the ruling group, which at different times was red or yellow or black or white, usually regarded the others as inferior.

Slave oppression had also existed in earlier times, but this was usually on the basis of military conquest and the conquerors—the ancient Greeks and Romans—did not develop a theory of racial superiority to rationalize their right to exploit their slaves.

Just as mankind, prior to the rise of capitalism, had not previously experienced an economic system which naturally and normally pursues the expansion of material productive forces at the expense of human forces, so it had never known a society which naturally and normally pursues the systematic exploitation and dehumanization of one race of people by another. An organic link between capitalism and racism is therefore certainly suggested.

The parallel between the rise of capitalism and the rise of racism has been traced by a number of scholars. The Portuguese, who were the first Europeans to come into contact with Africans at the end of the fifteenth and beginning of the sixteenth centuries, treated them as natural friends and allies. They found African customs strange and exotic but also found much to admire in their social and political organization, craftsmanship, architecture, and so on. At this point the chief technological advantages enjoyed by the Europeans were their navigation skills and firepower (both, by the way, originally learned from the Chinese). In the next four centuries these two advantages would be used to plunder four continents of their wealth in minerals and people and thereby to increase the technological superiority of Europeans by leaps and bounds.

Africa was turned into a hunting ground for slaves to work the land of the West Indies and the Southern colonies that had been stolen from the Indians. As the slave trade expanded, its enormous profits concentrated capital in Europe and America for the expansion of commerce, industry, and invention, while in Africa the social fabric was torn apart. In the Americas the blood and sweat of African slaves produced the sugar, tobacco, and later cotton to feed the refineries, distilleries, and textile mills, first of Western Europe and then of the Northern United States.

The more instrumental the slave trade in destroying African culture, the more those involved directly and indirectly in the slave traffic tried to convince themselves and others that there had never been any African culture in the first place. The more brutal the methods needed to enforce slavery against rebellious blacks, the more the brutalizers insisted that the submissiveness of slavery was the natural state of black people. The more valuable the labor of blacks to Southern agriculture, precisely because of the relatively advanced stage of agriculture in their African homeland, the more white Americans began to insist that they had done the African savage a favor by bringing him to a land where he could be civilized by agricultural labor. Thus, step by step, in order to justify their mutually reinforcing economic exploitation and forceful subjugation of blacks, living, breathing white Americans created a scientifically cloaked theory of white superiority and black inferiority.

In order to understand the ease with which racism entrenched itself in Europe and North America, it is important to emphasize that not only the big merchants, manufacturers, and shipowners benefited from the slave trade and slavery. All kinds of little people on both sides of the Atlantic drew blood money directly from the slave traffic. Thus, "though a large part of the Liverpool slave traffic was monopolized by about ten large firms, many of the small vessels in the trade were fitted out by attorneys, drapers, grocers, barbers, and tailors. The shares in the ventures were subdivided, one having one-eighth, another one-fifteenth, a third one-thirty-second part of a share and so on. . . . 'almost every order of people is interested in a Guinea cargo.' "[*]

The middle classes benefited indirectly from the general economic prosperity created by the slave trade. "Every port to which the slave ships returned saw the rise of manufactures in the eighteenth century—refineries, cottons, dyeworks, sweetmaking—in increasing numbers which testified to the advance of business and industry."[**] In the expanding economy the shopkeeper found a growing number of customers for his goods, the farmer for his produce, the doctor and lawyer for their skills.

To white workers at the very bottom of white society, African slavery also brought substantial benefits. First, the expanding industry made possible by the profits of slave trafficking created jobs at an expanding rate. Second, in the Americas particularly, white indentured servants were able to escape from the dehumanization of plantation servitude only because of the seemingly inexhaustible supply of constantly imported African slaves to take their place.

Contrary to racist mythology, blacks did not thrive any better in the rice swamps and on the sugar and cotton plantations than whites. Nor had blacks been treated significantly worse than white indentured servants in the early days of colonial settlement when convicts and poor whites, kidnapped off the wharfs of Liverpool and London, had been crowded onto dirty transatlantic ships en route to Southern plantations to work as white indentured servants. These whites had been bracketed with blacks and treated as "white trash." But they had one advantage denied the blacks: they were of the same color as their masters. Therefore, when their contracts expired or they were able to escape, they could not be easily detected, and, *because there were blacks to take their place*, the slave masters did not put out the great effort which would have been needed to capture them. Thus the ex-

---

[*] Eric Williams, *Capitalism and Slavery* (New York: G. P. Putnam, 1966).

[**] Ernest Mandel, *Marxist Economic Theory* (New York: Monthly Review Press, 1969), p. 111.

indentured servant climbed into the free society as farmer or worker on the backs of black slaves.

It is only when we understand this immediate economic and social stake which not only the slave owners and the capitalist entrepreneurs but the entire white population—including doctors, lawyers, bakers, and candlestickmakers (but not, of course, the Indian chiefs whose lands were taken for the plantations and farms)—had in the enslavement of blacks that we can understand the realities of racism in this country. Racism was real because there were real people with a stake in racism—racists—and these real people were ready to resort to force to protect their stake. As Eugene Genovese has pointed out, blacks were often safer on the slave plantation than off it because of the hostile, armed non-slaveholding whites.*

Radical historians have tended to underplay these realities, pointing out how, in the final analysis, slavery impoverished the soil, drove the free farmers farther West, kept down the wages of white workers, etc. This is because these historians, usually white, have begun their analysis with the plight of white workers in the process of capitalist production and then have tried to fit the grievances and revolt of blacks into this theoretical framework. Hence, like the Kerner commissioners, they have failed to prepare us for the surfacing of white racist workers. Also, addressing themselves chiefly to white workers and trying to convince these workers of the need to destroy capitalism, they have insisted that black and white workers are "really" (i.e., according to their theory) allies, kept apart only by a vertical color line which the evil slave owners and capitalists have conspired to draw down the middle between them.

The historical fact is that without African slavery the class struggle between capitalists and workers could not even have been joined in the first place. For the capitalist, it served the functions of primitive accumulation. That is, it provided both the

---

* Eugene Genovese, *The Legacy of Slavery and the Roots of Black Nationalism,* a speech delivered at the 1966 Socialist Scholars Conference and reprinted by the New England Free Press.

initial capital *and* the labor force freed from the means of production which is a prerequisite for the process of capitalist accumulation inside the factory.*

For the individual white indentured servant or laborer, African slavery meant the opportunity to rise above the status of slave and become farmer or free laborer. Thus, early in the history of this country a pattern was created which persists to this day: physical and social mobility for white workers into and within increasingly modernized industries, possible only because there is a reserve army of black labor to scavenge the dirty, unskilled jobs in the fields and sweatshops.

Instead of the vertical color line dreamed up by white radicals, there has actually existed a horizontal platform resting on the backs of blacks and holding them down, while on top white workers have been free to move up the social and economic ladder of advancing capitalism. This horizontal platform, a ceiling for blacks and a floor for whites, has created and maintained a black labor force serving the economic needs of advancing capitalism, as it has developed, stage by stage, from manufacturing capitalism to industrial capitalism to monopoly capitalism to its present stage of military-industrial capitalism, or what is more popularly known as the "military-industrial complex."

Capitalist production is unlike all previous exploitative eco-

---

* "In themselves, money and commodities are not more capital than are the means of production and of subsistence. They want transforming into capital. But this transformation can only take place under certain circumstances that centre in this, viz., that two very different kinds of commodity-possessors must come face to face and into contact; on the one hand, the owners of money, means of production, means of subsistence, who are eager to increase the sum of values they possess, by buying other people's labor power; on the other hand, free laborers, the sellers of their own labor-power and therefore the sellers of labor. Free laborers, in the double sense that neither they themselves form part and parcel of the means of production, as in the case of slaves, bondsmen, etc., nor do the means of production belong to them, as in the case of peasant-proprietors; they are, therefore, free from, unencumbered by, any means of production of their own. With this polarization of the market for commodities, the fundamental conditions of capitalist production are given." ("The Secret of Primitive Accumulation," *Capital*, Vol. I, p. 785.)

nomic systems. In previous exploitative societies the ruling classes consumed the proceeds of exploitation in lavish personal living, including an ever expanding personal retinue, or in the purchase of more land and slaves. Under capitalism, on the other hand, the major part of the profits derived from the exploitation of labor is reinvested in new and more advanced means of production. This, the essential law of motion of capitalism, is known as capitalist accumulation. Constant expansion and modernization of the means of production, made possible by the exploitation of labor, have now become the driving force of the system.

The results of capitalist accumulation are all around us. Constant revolutionizing of production, ceaselessly advancing technology, mammoth factories and, controlling this gigantic accumulation of industrial plant and fluid (finance) capital, an ever diminishing number of interlocking corporations and individuals.

With increasing investment in modern equipment has come the increasing productivity of labor and therefore a constantly decreasing proportion of capital invested in labor compared to that invested in machinery. This value composition of capital, changing along with changing technology, is called the organic composition of capital.

A hundred years ago Karl Marx pointed out the internal contradictions inherent in the changing organic composition of capital. One of the chief contradictions, he pointed out, is the fall in the rate of profit as less and less capital is invested in labor (variable capital) compared to that invested in machinery (constant capital). This is because only the capital invested in human labor can produce varying quantities of surplus value, depending on how long or how hard you work the workers. That is why Marx called it variable capital, in contrast to the constant capital invested in machinery whose value is simply transferred into the finished product on a *pro rata* basis.

Closer to common experience, this contradiction expresses itself as the difficulty in maintaining the value of existing capital—i.e., that already invested in means of production—when newer and more modern means of production are constantly being created. How can the relatively obsolete machines and factories be kept in production, producing profit, so that the total social capital available for modernization will not be reduced because of the building of new plants? This is what Marx called the *general* contradiction of capitalism.*

Advancing capitalism has been able to counteract these contradictions only by using the colonized people in Latin America, Africa, Asia, and inside the United States itself.

In the late nineteenth century, in order to counteract the decline in the rate of profit, monopoly capitalism began to export "surplus capital" to what we today call the Third World. This exported capital was surplus in the sense that in the colonies it did not have to be invested in the same growing ratio between constant and variable capital as it had in the imperialist fatherland. The capital invested in the colonies could be used to extract surplus value from a work force prevented by the military power of a colonial administration from organizing for better working conditions, shorter hours, higher wages. Finally, the surplus profits thus extracted from the colonial work force were not reinvested in the colonies but were sent home to add to the total social capital available for modernization in the oppressing country. In this way the colonial countries were systematically kept in a state of undevelopment in order to accelerate economic development at home.

An analogous process has taken place within the borders of the United States, where the black work force has been used as a colonial work force to preserve the value of existing capital.

The role which blacks were to play in this process was fixed after Reconstruction when blacks were kept on the cotton plantations not only by the brute force of Southern planters and sheriffs but by the violent hostility of white workers to their entry into the advancing industries of the North and South. Between 1880 and 1890 alone there were fifty strikes in the North against the employment of black workers in industry. The result was that in 1910 the number of blacks in industries other than cotton production was less than 0.5 percent, while as late as 1930, 68.75 percent of gainfully employed blacks were still in agriculture and domestic service.

---

* *Capital*, Vol. III, p. 292.

As blacks began to move into the cities in this country, white workers acted as the principal human agent assisting American capitalism to counteract the fundamental contradiction between constantly advancing technology and the need to maintain the value of existing plant. They have done so by collectively and often forcibly restricting blacks to technologically less advanced industries or to what is known as "common labor" inside the modern plant or in construction. A perfect example of the system in operation on the job has been in the building industry. "The black man digs a ditch. Then the white man steps in and lays the pipes and the black man covers the ditch. The black man cleans the tank and then the white boilermaker comes on and makes the repairs."*

This is the scavenger role in production which white workers, acting *consciously* on behalf of their own social mobility and *unconsciously* on behalf of constantly advancing capitalism, have assigned to blacks and other colored peoples, such as the Chinese and Japanese on the West Coast, and the Mexicans and Puerto Ricans.

But the scavenger role has not been restricted to jobs. In the same way that blacks have been forced to take on the old sub-standard jobs, disdained and discarded by socially mobile whites, they have been confined to used homes, used schools, used churches, and used stores. (Only in the matter of the most ephemeral consumer goods—cars, deoderants, hair spray, clothing, etc.—are they able and in fact encouraged to buy the latest models.) For the used homes and churches they make excessive payments which add to the total capital available to the entire economy for new buildings, new plants, new churches, new homes. As in the days of primitive accumulation, the entire white community benefits, not only from the direct receipt of interest and principal on these homes and churches but in terms of new industries with their streamlined buildings and their increasingly skilled jobs.

The situation has reached its climax in the role assigned by the

---

* Sterling D. Spero and Abram L. Harris, *The Black Worker* (New York: Atheneum, 1968).

military-industrial state to young blacks on the frontlines of Vietnam. The disproportionate number of black youth fighting and dying to preserve the system in Asia makes it possible for an increasing number of white youth to attend college and be prepared for the new industries of the future. The systematic undevelopment of the black community is thus the foundation for the systematic development of the white community.

The economic advantages to the United States of having a colony inside its own borders have been tremendous. By using the colonial force of blacks, U.S. capitalism has been able to moderate the general contradiction of capitalist accumulation. That is to say, it has been able to accelerate technological expansion and at the same time keep profits coming in from continuing exploitation of its obsolescent, "used" factories, homes, schools, stores, etc. As a result, the United States has developed into the technologically most advanced country in the world.

But the human costs of this counteracting of internal economic contradictions have been equally tremendous. On the one hand, for the sake of American economic development, 20 to 30 million blacks and thousands of black communities across the country have paid the high cost of economic backwardness. As I noted earlier, "Their present stage of decay, decline, and dilapidation—their present stage of undevelopment—is a product of capitalist exploitation. They have been used and re-used to produce profit by every form of capitalist: landlords, construction industries, merchants, insurance brokers, bankers, finance companies, racketeers, and manufacturers of cars, appliances, steel, and every kind of industrial commodity."

Less obvious but increasingly dangerous has been the human price paid by the entire country for advancing capitalism by all means necessary. In the course of making America a unique land of opportunity in which whites climb up the social and economic ladder on the backs of blacks, the American people have become the most materialistic, the most opportunistic, the most individualistic—in sum, the most politically and socially irresponsible people in the world. Step by step, choice by choice, year after year, decade after decade, they have become the political victims of the system they themselves created, unable to make political decisions on the basis of principle no matter how crucial the issue. So long have they evaded the question of right and wrong that the question of what is right and what is wrong now evades them. Thus, while counteracting the economic contradictions of capitalism, the American people have come up against an even more dangerous, even graver contradiction in capitalism, the contradiction between being the technologically most advanced and the politically most backward people in the world.

The American political system, based upon two barely distinguishable political parties, is a structural manifestation of this backwardness. In other advanced countries the workers formed political parties of labor early in this century. These parties, despite their obvious shortcomings (especially their failure to create a revolutionary alternative to fascism), nevertheless served not only to represent the economic and social interests of labor but also to educate the entire country in some sense of social and political consciousness. In the United States, however, all efforts to create a political party of the working classes, particularly in the late nineteenth century and in the 1930's, have come to naught because white workers have focused on the individual's opportunity to climb into the middle class. The result is that the political process has been reduced to a meaningless ritual whose mechanics and outcome are decided by Madison Avenue hucksters.

The manifestations of this contradiction between economic overdevelopment and political underdevelopment are everywhere. The chickens have really come home to roost. Unable to subordinate material values to human values, the United States is consistently unable to put politics in command over economics or to choose men over weapons. Twenty-five years ago it could not resist dropping atom bombs on the Japanese people. Today it cannot resist dropping napalm in Vietnam or manufacturing it for use against other peoples struggling for liberation, particularly in Africa. Its universities, professed centers for the Humanities, are being turned into arsenals of research into the most advanced means for destroying humanity. Its cities are being transformed into parking spaces, its highways into poison gas chambers by a ceaselessly expanding auto industry, its lakes and rivers into catch-basins for industrial waste. Successive administrations, Republican and Democrat alike, know that the United States cannot win the genocidal war in Vietnam and that virtually the whole world and its own youth see no distinction between its behavior and that of Hitler. At home the country is coming apart at the seams. Yet white, moderate, responsible America cannot mobilize the political will to get out of Vietnam.

Inside the United States this contradiction is equally devastating. Faced with the civil war conditions created by the black revolt, "white moderate responsible America" continues to try to meet the crisis with the same methods and the same philosophy which created the crisis in the first place. Thus the Kerner Commission, far from suggesting any fundamental change in the system of white labor mobility on the backs of blacks, proposes its continuation. In outlining its crash program for the black hard-core, the Commission explicitly states:

> We do not intend with our program for the hard-core disadvantaged to stimulate the "leap-frogging" by the hard-core unemployed of the other two groups. Certainly the already employed must not lose their jobs in order to make room for the hard-core unemployed. Only a program which both *upgrades* the already employed and *thereby* creates openings for the hard-core, can satisfy this need. (*Emphasis added.*)

In other words, blacks are to remain scavengers.

At the same time the Kerner Commission predictably proposes bringing a few blacks into the system at a higher level, as black capitalists, black project directors, black administrators, etc. These black collaborators, like the African rulers who recruited their own people for the slave traders, or the "house niggers" and drivers who identified with "old Massa" on the plantation, or the black elite today governing the neo-colonies in Africa, are then supposed to have enough of a stake in the operation of the system to cooperate in pacification programs against their black brothers and sisters. Ultimately these black collaborators are being programmed for the same role in suppressing black revolt which the South Vietnamese government has been set up to play in relation to the Vietnamese people.

Unfortunately for these "white moderate responsible Americans," but fortunately for the future of humanity, this program for perpetuating the system of scavengers and collaborators is doomed to failure. This is not only because the black revolt has already advanced too far for blacks to accept being put back into their place at the bottom of the ladder. It is also because of the counter-revolt which is now growing by leaps and bounds among white workers and white administrators who feel themselves threatened by the black upheaval beneath them and by the concessions which the white power structure seems inclined to make to those "uppity niggers." The real living breathing racists whose existence was ignored by the Kerner Commission refuse to be ignored. Conscious of increasing automation and cybernation and imbued with the conviction that labor mobility should be the basis of increasing status and increasing income, regardless of what happens to anybody else, white workers regard the upgrading of every black man or woman as an immediate danger to their jobs and to their most sacrosanct principles. Likewise, the white middle classes—especially the school principals, teachers, policemen, social workers, and other white collar workers who have been receiving high salaries for the "dirty work" of administering the black colony—feel increasingly threatened by the demand for black control of the black community. Together these white workers and middle-class administrators, calling themselves the "forgotten Americans," constitute a growing counter-revolutionary force, threatening not only the black community but also all those "white moderate responsible Americans" who are so high on the social and economic ladder that they do not feel threatened by minor concessions to black America.

The chief value of the Kerner report is that it has exposed, to all those willing to look, the counter-revolutionary dangers inherent in trying to end racism and at the same time maintain the economic and social system inseparable from it.

As long as the economic system of expansion by all means necessary (i.e., capitalism) and the philosophy corresponding to this system (i.e., materialism, individualism, and opportunism) continue to exist, this country will continue to produce a working class which is racist, i.e., determined to maintain its economic and social mobility at the expense of blacks.

To succeed in destroying racism in this country, the revolutionary movement must overthrow the practice of putting economics in command of politics, which has been the governing principle of American development, and replace it with the practice of putting politics in command of economics, which is the essence of *today's* social revolutions the world over.

Before politics can be put in command of economics, power must be taken away from those living, breathing Americans who have governed and continue to govern this country according to the system of economic expansion by all means necessary.

Black people in the United States are the ones who have been most economically undeveloped by the American economic system, but at the same time they have been forced by the racism inseparable from the system to become more concerned with human values than with material values. Racism and capitalism have also concentrated them into a social force, situated at the heart of the major cities of this country and conscious of their common oppression as black people. Hence blacks are the ones best suited to lead the struggle for the revolutionary power necessary to put politics in command of economics.

Not only is this the only way to destroy racism in the United States. It is also the only way to solve what has become the essential contradiction in this country, the contradiction between economic overdevelopment and political underdevelopment.

*1969*

# 13

# The American
# Revolution:
# Putting Politics
# in Command

In 1963 I concluded my first book with these words:

> If the leap that the American people have to take in order to
> meet the problems of this new age of abundance were not so great,
> the powers of the secret police would likewise not be so great. In
> the 30's the problems were relatively simple. All that was required
> was that the poor struggle against the rich, who were the capital-
> ists and whose failure was clear and obvious.
>
> Today in the 60's, the struggle is much more difficult. What it
> requires is that people in every stratum of the population clash not
> only with the agents of the silent police state but with their own
> prejudices, their own outmoded ideas, their own fears which keep
> them from grappling with the new realities of our age. The American
> people must find a way to insist upon their own right and responsi-
> bility to make political decisions and to determine policy in all
> spheres of social existence—whether it is foreign policy, the work
> process, education, race relations, or community life. The coming
> struggle is a political struggle to take political power out of the
> hands of the few and put it in the hands of the many. But in order
> to get this power into the hands of the many, it will be necessary
> for the many not only to fight the powerful few but to fight and
> clash among themselvs as well.

Today, as we begin a new decade, the conflict between the
social forces needed to drive the revolution forward has advanced
far beyond our wildest expectations. Seven years ago the idea of
a twentieth-century American Revolution was so remote that most
people assumed that the title of my book, *The American Revolution,* referred to events 200 years ago. Now, side by side with the
growth of irreconcilable social forces, the headaches of daily
life in America have become so intolerable that the question is

no longer whether there will be an American Revolution but rather what it means, when and if it will be over, and what kind of new society it will produce.

Every problem which confronted the United States in the early 1960's has become not only infinitely more complex but infinitely more demanding of solution and decision by the American people.

The war in Southeast Asia is not just a military war. It is an international political struggle in which the traditional and systematic use by the United States of its advanced technology to determine the economic, social, and political destinies of the world's peoples is being contested and defeated. Moreover, each setback to the counter-revolutionary policies of this country (in China, Korea, Cuba, and Vietnam) has only served to accelerate the growth of a *New International* of developing nations, representing a revolutionary humanist social force of billions, a force which the United States cannot destroy short of atomic warfare powerful enough to destroy the entire planet. Faced with this reality, the American people must decide whether, in order to preserve their own system, they are now prepared to accept a state of permanent war against the majority of the world's peoples (mostly colored) and the garrisoning of American troops in over fifty countries of the world as an integral part of the American "way of life," in the same way and for many of the same reasons that a hundred years ago they accepted racism as an integral part of the American way of life.

Labor, once the most important means to expand production and consumption, has become increasingly expendable as the profits derived from its exploitation have been reinvested in advancing technology. This technology in turn has made the remaining labor so monotonous and fragmented that it is more worthy of robots than of human beings. The result is that a growing number of people, both in and out of work, are beginning to question the purpose of labor and the validity of the prevailing philosophy that man should live only by the sweat of his brow.

In American schools and universities, amid turmoil and growing tensions, it is becoming increasingly clear that the American system of education, dedicated to the increase of earning power and representing an investment of many billions of dollars and

the full-time occupation of some fifty million people, is a failure
and that the basic purpose of education itself must be rede-
termined.

With a big question mark over the value of both labor and
education, courts, jails, and prisons all over the country have now
become so crowded with those charged with anti-social activities
that none of these institutions can any longer claim to be deter-
rents to crime, let alone agencies of rehabilitation. Instead, the
courts, the jails, and the prisons are now generally acknowledged
to be key links in a system by which youthful delinquents are
transformed into hardened criminals. Instead of protecting society
from the criminal, these institutions have become fertilizers for
the crimes which most threaten society.

In every city and across the country the very environment
which has made possible man's progress and survival for thousands of years is being polluted so rapidly by the waste and
residue of today's unlimited mass production that ecologists are
seriously discussing the possibility of life disappearing on this
planet before the end of the twentieth century. Closely related
to the destruction of the natural and social environment by industrial and consumer waste is its steady demolition to serve the
needs of private transportation. With rapid public transportation
disappearing because the jobs and profits of the auto industry
require the encouragement of private transportation, parking and
driving space for private chariots has been given unquestioned
priority over living and breathing space for human beings. The
result is that the earth is being turned into an asphalt jungle and
the atmosphere into smog.

Overwhelmed by the problems created by industrial technology, society will soon be faced with the even more complex
issues arising out of bio-technology, which brings with it the
power of a few to create masses of superhuman or subhuman
beings.

Frustrated by their inability to cope with problems that have
become insoluble on an individual basis but still hoping for an
individual solution, millions of people seek escape in all sorts of
drugs—from tranquilizers to heroin—pushed at them from all
directions: on the TV screen, in the poolroom, and on the street

corner. At the head of this legal and illegal drug traffic are both organized crime and an equally unscrupulous drug industry which, in the interests of profit, has helped transform the world's wealthiest nation into one of its unhealthiest. Increasing drug addiction has brought in its wake increasing crime to feed drug habits, until no street, day or night, is safe for the ordinary pedestrian. Thus America has also become one of the world's most dangerous societies.

Meanwhile, the contradiction between the humane pretensions of this society and its actual anti-human practices, particularly to blacks inside the country and to billions of colored people outside, has become increasingly intolerable not only to blacks but to young whites, leading to increasing revolt, increasing rebellion, and increasingly violent talk and action, in the streets and on the campuses.

The result is that alienation, confusion, uncertainty, frustration, hopelessness, anger, fear, and desperation pervade every section of the population as it feels its traditional beliefs crumbling and as it witnesses the assassination, in full public view, of one after another of those who promise leadership out of the wilderness of demoralization and powerlessness. Not even the landing of men on the moon last July—the greatest technical achievement in earthman's history—could restore this country's confidence in itself. Even before the first giant step had been taken on the moon, the debate as to the value and purpose of the exploit had begun to rage on earth; not only on the air waves where all could hear, but in the privacy of each man's doubts.

Faced with division inside the country, all levels of a government which formerly claimed to referee the conflicting interests of different sections of the population now increasingly resort to physical force and open psychological manipulation to mobilize their supporters against their critics. The police forces, from J. Edgar Hoover's on down, take on the functions of political organizations, openly dedicated to the preservation of white supremacy and the American way of life, more concerned with protecting the status quo from radical ideas and organizations than with protecting society from organized crime. By its deliberate efforts to muddy up the fundamental distinction between political activity and crime, the federal government itself is fostering disrespect for the judicial process, inciting to riot and murder, and unleashing the most reactionary forces in the nation. With every passing day its illegitimacy becomes more transparent.

In this crisis more and more people are beginning to feel that only a revolution can bring them release from their fears and anxieties. It is not difficult to feel. The difficulty comes in attempting to make the feeling concrete. This is not surprising since when we talk about a revolution in the United States we are talking about a revolution for which there is no historical precedent. History has nothing to tell us about a revolution in a country where so large a proportion of the population has materially benefited from the system even while being exploited by it and therefore feels that its own interest is bound up with the active defense of the system.

When people talk about a revolution, the first model that usually comes to mind is the Russian Revolution. Remembering only the period from February to October 1917, most people think of the Russian Revolution as a hurricane which moved rapidly from the collapse of the old regime in the face of military defeat to the seizure of power by the Bolsheviks, all within an eight-month period.

Another model that comes to the popular mind is that of the Cuban Revolution. In this case, most people think of the landing of the "Gramma" in 1956 followed by three relatively short years of guerrilla fighting by a small armed force in the mountains and then the victorious march on Havana in 1959.

Finally, there are the models of the Chinese and Vietnamese revolutions, involving long years of protracted struggle through which the great masses of people were transformed into new kinds of socially conscious, socially responsible human beings, their will to struggle and their vision escalated through escalating conflicts over issues affecting their daily lives.

Whatever their differences, all these revolutions had in common the fact that they took place in economically undeveloped countries. In each of these countries the consciousness of economic backwardness compared to that of the Western nations and the consciousness of the urgent need for economic development pervaded the entire population and was a crucial factor in unifying the majority of people behind the revolution and driving it forward despite innumerable setbacks.

When we come to the United States, however, there is no urgency about economic development, either to meet the material needs of the people or to compete with other nations. The United States excels in the economic arena. It is not a feudal or semi-developed colonialized land; nor is it threatened by military defeat at home or by an alien power from abroad.

The first question that has to be answered, therefore, is whether there is any arena in which the United States urgently needs revolutionary—that is to say, rapid and fundamental—development and reorganization. The answer is unequivocally yes. But, unlike the nations of Africa, Asia, and Latin America, the arena in which this country needs revolutionary change is not the *economic* but the *political,* not the *material* but the *social.* The essential, the key, contradiction in the United States that must be resolved if this country is to survive is the contradiction between economic overdevelopment and political underdevelopment.

The urgent, crying need of the American people is to undergo a fundamental transformation from the individualists and materialists they are today into a new breed of socially and politically conscious and responsible human beings. Instead of being concerned only with their own material advancement and satisfied with the political decisions of the military-industrial-academic complex as long as these expand production and consumption, the American people must be dragged, pulled, pushed into situations where they are compelled to make socially responsible decisions—until the energy, the skill, and the will to make such decisions have become second nature.

Such a radical transformation in hundreds of millions of persons, difficult under any circumstances, seems almost impossible in a country that was founded on the extermination of one race of people, the Indian, and the enslavement of another, the African. From the very beginning of this nation, the behavior pattern of subordinating human to economic values has been systematically inculcated into the people by precept and by practice. After the Civil War it was not difficult for whites, from the highest to the lowest, to accept the virtual re-enslavement of blacks, despite constitutional measures guaranteeing their freedom, since this guaranteed a labor supply for the dirty work on the Southern cotton plantations which nourished the Northern textile industry, and at the same time made jobs in expanding industry available to immigrant whites.

Economic development has been the reason for the super-exploitation of blacks at every stage, and the super-exploitation of blacks has in turn accelerated economic development. Thus the American way of life has been created, a life of expanding comfort and social mobility for whites, based upon servitude and lack of freedom for blacks. This in turn has encouraged everyone to look upon everyone else as a steppingstone to personal advancement.

In the course of creating this system the country has become the technologically most advanced country in the world, but it has also become a nation so dedicated to technological advancement that its citizens systematically evade any political decisions that might interfere with their personal economic interest. Thus the United States has become a nation which is as backward in political and social decision-making as most new nations are in technological decision-making. The American people have been going along with whatever advanced their own immediate material interests for so long that they have no interest or practice in evaluating and deciding political issues. Except for those unions that functioned briefly in the 1930's as mass social and political assemblies for the working class, Americans have created no structure, no apparatus, within which they can fight over the issues and grievances of their daily lives or those of their communities and their country, coming to decisions for which they can be held responsible.

The essence of the American way of life has been and continues to be the organization of all institutions to achieve the most rapid economic development, and this in turn is expected to solve all the problems of the society. Now, however, it is clear that economic development has created as many problems as it has solved. The United States is a society in which there is an increasing investment in highly advanced technology and an increasing concentration of economic and political power in the hands of a few individuals and corporations who control this vast technological apparatus. But accompanying this rapid techno- logical development and the concentration of skills and power at one pole, there has been a systematic and continuous decline in skills, responsibility, and participation at the other pole, particu- larly at the very bottom of the ladder among the blacks, Mexican- Americans, Puerto Ricans, Indians, etc. At the same time, because of the reliance on economic development to solve all social prob- lems, no institutions or procedures exist to bring about the rapid political development needed to cope with rapid technological and social change.

Thus we have arrived—not because of the malice of any par- ticular individual or group but as the climax of the natural de- velopment of the system—at the present dangerous situation where the American people, with the techniques to destroy or advance mankind at their disposal, do not have the political will or consciousness to choose one rather than the other.

The American system has been able to arrive at its present stage because the majority of the population (white) accepted the philosophy of economic development as the key to social progress. They did not question it because, on the whole, they have benefited from it. The chief victims have been blacks, who stayed at the bottom scavenging white leavings, until recently too convinced of their own inferiority to rebel.

As long as blacks did not dream of reaching the middle or top rungs of the American economic and social ladder, they were no threat to the system. But sixteen years ago, precisely at the time when the number of positions on the middle and lower rungs of the ladder was declining because of automation and cybernation, blacks began to feel and believe in their right to equality. Com- peting with whites for higher positions, they have aroused the fury of whites for disturbing what whites have wanted to believe was a perfect society. Actually, by making themselves visible blacks have only been exposing the bankruptcy of a system which has put economics in command of politics and has failed to de- velop the politics that can command economics.

In disrupting the smooth operations of the system, blacks are also revealing to themselves the inseparable and antagonistic relation between their own undevelopment and lack of freedom and the system's freedom to develop. It is impossible for blacks to free or develop themselves without turning over every institution of this society, each of which has been structured with blacks at the bottom. The present situation only brings to a climax the insoluble contradictions in a system which has developed freely through the enforced underdevelopment of one group of people. Today 35 to 50 percent of black young people are unemployed and roaming the streets, their only future a prison cell or a rice paddy in Southeast Asia. Automation and cybernation have made the unskilled, undeveloped labor of our young men and women increasingly expendable. Displaced from the land and concentrated in the slums of the nation's cities, we are no longer needed as producers. Yet we are constantly urged by the mass media to become consumers in order to keep the mass production lines of America operating at full capacity, even if we can only get the wherewithal for such consumption by one or another form of hustling. Hence at the end of the road for millions of our people looms only a prison cell.

It is only from this realistic appraisal of the organic interrelationship between our role as black people and the economic system that a perspective for revolutionary struggle can be developed. No longer needed in a structure which has been created to meet the needs of rapid economic development even at the cost of exterminating human beings, we face extermination unless we can revolutionize the ends and means of the entire society.

Blacks, and particularly young blacks, are the revolutionary social force inside this country, the only social force in irreversible motion. Yet blacks have not faced the need for the revolutionary political theory and political organization that they must develop in order to give political leadership to the task of revolutionizing the entire society. This is because blacks are also a part and product of the country's political undevelopment. They are reluctant to tackle the responsibilities of revolutionary politics because they too share in the American tendency to evade reality, hoping to find simple solutions for very complex problems.

In the last sixteen years the black movement has tested and

explored many different solutions to the problems of black people in this country, from mass demonstrations to mass rebellion, from voting black to buying black. In the course of many activities, the movement has produced a tremendous social force of millions of black people, formerly apathetic and apolitical but now anxious to act. At the same time the movement has rid itself of a number of illusions: the illusion that integration in and of itself is the solution; or that non-violence or violence in themselves are the solution; or that spontaneous eruptions in and of themselves are the solution; or that militant rhetoric is the solution; or that the unity of sheer numbers is the solution. It is now clear that the problems of black people cannot be solved by the most charismatic or most militant spokesmen for black grievances, or by economic aid from city, state, or federal governments, or by massive programs for hiring the hard-core unemployed.

Faced with these realities, the black movement is now painfully evaluating its past actions and seeking a program for the future. In the meantime the revolutionary momentum of the black movement has brought into the social arena a white counter-revolutionary force which feels certain that its entire way of life is threatened and that it must wipe out the black movement before it acquires any more momentum. Unlike the black revolutionary forces, the counter-forces do not have to search for an ideology before they can plot their actions. Their ideology is that of the existing society: materialism, individualism, opportunism. Even if, as white workers and middle classes, they do not reap all the benefits from this system, even if they are powerless to affect its major decisions about what to produce or when to go to war, they still believe that it is the best system in the world because it is the system which has enabled them as whites to climb up and over any blacks. It has therefore become for them a system of privilege worth defending at all costs.

The present cry for "law and order" and the prevailing police terror in black communities are not just some conspiracy dreamed up by a few right-wing policemen and Minutemen and then foisted upon the masses of whites. They are a reflection of what most whites expect and demand from their police force in order to preserve the American way of life.

It is because blacks can see this growing counter-revolutionary force all around them that so many tendencies have developed inside the black movement during the past few years. Most of these tendencies are attempts to escape the cold realities of the American economic system and the protracted struggle necessary to revolutionize America that are the price of black freedom. Among the various solutions to the dilemma of black people in America which are offered or advocated at the present time are: 1) return to Africa; 2) set up separate states; 3) black control of black communities, leaving the task of changing the "mother country" to whites; 4) black cultural separation; and 5) black capitalism. There are even large numbers of blacks who still believe that they can be assimilated into this society as the old immigrant groups were if only they can elect some more black politicians. Most of these tendencies are led by and reflect the interests of various sections of the black middle classes—the professionals, artists, preachers, businessmen, and politicians. All of these consider themselves part of the Black Power movement that has dominated the black revolt in the wake of the Watts, Newark, and Detroit rebellions; and each, with its particular goal, has some support within the black community. Each believes that if the black masses would support its particular solution, the black problem would be solved and the black revolution would have succeeded. Black militants, and particularly black youth, drift restlessly between these organizations, attracted "wherever the action is," not particularly concerned about the practicality of any particular goal. Meanwhile, large numbers of older blacks still maintain a lingering hope for integration, despite the fact that the manifest failure of integration was what originally gave birth to the mass rebellions and the Black Power movement.

Whatever may be the present shortcomings of the black movement, it has created the largest concentration of revolutionary social forces that this country has ever known. It has also created an unprecedented level of mass political development and of mass effort to find the correct solution to real social problems. Within this unprecedented political force there exists the potential for mass political consciousness and for revolutionary struggle on a level never before achieved in this country.

The revolutionary leadership of black people inside this country is presently at the black nationalist stage; the conception of Black Power is still within the black nationalist framework. Black people have recognized that there is a uniqueness about their history and about their present condition which sets them apart from the rest of the people inside the United States. They have also recognized that this, the basis of their oppression, is also a source of strength. Such a sense of nationalism could only have been achieved as a result of a long process of continuing struggle which has forced blacks to give up certain myths: that they can ever become like white people, or that it would be desirable to become like white people, or that they will ever be free as long as they are ruled by white power. The protracted struggle of the last sixteen years, with its minor victories and its many failures and setbacks, has not only swelled the ranks of the black movement; it has given blacks a sense of their uniqueness and their identity as a nation of people.

Black nationalism is and has been progressive because it has bound black people together and given them strength, but black nationalism in and of itself is not a sufficient answer to the problems of black people. Black people will have to go beyond the stage of black nationalism into the stage of black revolutionary nationalism if they are going to resolve the very real problems of black people. Only black revolutionary nationalism will enable them to attack the real causes of their problems. Black nationalism has created a united black consciousness, but a black consciousness which does not develop into a real and realistic attack on the causes of black oppression can only become a false consciousness, a breeding ground for the cultism, adventurism, and opportunism which are rampant in the movement. Black revolutionary nationalism involves real and realistic programs of struggle not only against those who control the very real institutions of this society, but also to reorganize these institutions to make them serve human needs rather than the need of the economic system for profit and technological development.

The first step in the development of nationalism inside a colony in Africa, Asia, or Latin America is usually very simple: it is to oust the colonial oppressor. The second step is much more difficult because it requires a rapid political development of the people, enabling them to bring about a drastic reorganization of the economic and political system. If this rapid political development does not take place simultaneously with the struggle for national independence—or immediately thereafter—the new nation will soon sink back into neo-colonialism. This is what has happened with most of the African colonies. This is what Sekou Touré in Guinea and Amilcar Cabral in Guinea-Bissau are striving to avoid by concentrating on the political transformation of their people side by side with the struggle against the colonial oppressor.

In the United States the problem for blacks is much more complex because our lives and our condition are so bound up with those of the oppressor. On the one hand, we have lived a separate and distinct life. On the other, we have been an organic—an indispensable and intrinsic—part of the development of the most highly industrialized country in the world. Even while we have been systematically denied all the benefits of rapid industrialization, we have first been the direct source of the profits by which the country could industrialize itself rapidly and then been made superfluous by the results of this rapid industrialization. It is thus impossible to separate the development of our conditions of life as blacks in this country from the development of the system itself. Nor is it possible for blacks to free themselves without turning over every institution of this society.

The Black Power movement must recognize that if this society is ever going to be changed to meet the needs of black people, then Black Power will have to resolve the problems of the society as a whole and not just those of black people. In other words, Black Power cannot evade tackling all the problems of this society, because at the root of all the problems of black people is the same structure and the same system which is at the root of all the problems of all the people.

Even though blacks in the United States have many of the characteristics of a colonial people (super-exploited, undeveloped, powerless, segregated), there is no point in anyone, black or white, dealing or not dealing with the black movement as if blacks were in Asia or Africa. It is true that blacks must get themselves together before they can give leadership to whites. But even while they are getting themselves together, blacks cannot evade the questions that make a revolution in the United States essential. Nor can the white movement evade the fact that blacks constitute the vanguard for revolutionary struggle in this country and try to go its own way, just because whites are not accepted into black organizations. The fact that blacks are inside the United States, not in Africa or Asia or Latin America, is the specific historical condition of the American Revolution that black *and* white revolutionaries must face. Revolutionary-minded whites who try to evade this real historical condition are tempted to actions which provide an outlet chiefly for their psychological need to be "revolutionary." Revolutionary blacks who insist on ignoring the existence of whites in this society begin to build a fantasy realm in which all blacks can be judged to be brothers on the basis of color rather than on the basis of politics.

It is difficult for the Black Power movement to face this fact because, unlike the King movement, which was trying to reform the total society and provide leadership for both black and white, the Black Power movement, developing in reaction to the failure of integration and of the King movement, has confined itself to seeking a solution only for blacks, deliberately closing its eyes to the fact that the black condition is the result of a system whose influence and domination blacks cannot escape as long as the system continues to exist.

Confronted with such questions, the first declaration of most black groups today is: "We are not concerned about whites." The question is not whether blacks ought to be concerned about whites; it is whether blacks *can* solve their own problems without solving those of the total society and therefore those of whites. King's fundamental mistake was not his willingness to give leadership to whites as well as blacks. It was his illusion that whites could be reformed by moral appeals and that the American way of life can be reformed when it must be totally revolutionized—which can only be done by taking power away from whites. The growing problems of both the black and the white movement cannot be resolved until Black Power assumes the responsibility of leadership of the American Revolution as a whole.

This is not to propose inter-racial organization and activity, such as during the period of the integration movement. But if and when the Black Power movement accepts the awesome responsibility for revolutionizing this whole country, it will not have to spend so much of its time evading the question of what will happen to white people under Black Power. It will be able to put behind it the present psycho-social preoccupation with black-white relationships and recognize that sooner or later it will have to assume the responsibility for giving political direction to white revolutionaries who remain an auxiliary force because they lack a community with which to interact and develop in struggle. Most important, the movement will be able to devote its time and energy to the task whose time has come: the task of developing a black revolutionary leadership with the ideology, the perspective, the vision, and the program to win the Black Power necessary to revolutionize America.*

The first task of the developing revolution in the United States is to benefit black people who have the greatest need and the greatest concentration of social forces for this revolution; but the changes that this revolution will bring will benefit all but the small minority—as indeed every revolution must do. The peasants and workers in China were the ones with the most urgent need for revolution; hence it was from their needs and their mobilization that the fundamental perspective and program of the revolution were determined. But the Chinese revolutionary leaders did not spend their time worrying about whether or not other sections of Chinese society might also benefit from the revolution or whether they should utilize other sections of the population in the revolutionary struggle. They assumed, as every revolutionary leader must, that the entire society would benefit. They were concerned, as every revolutionary leader must be, to use every possible section of the society for the purpose of defeating the existing regime and building a new society.

The essence of revolutionary leadership is the ability to give to those social forces with the most urgent need for fundamental social change a vision of a new society in which they will be in

---

* See "The Role of the Vanguard Party," *Monthly Review*, April 1970.

a position to make the changes so vital to their needs. Mere awareness of their oppression and exploitation is not enough; they must be convinced that their present condition is unnecessary (hence that the present system is illegitimate), and that revolutionary struggles will enable them to solve a wide variety of the ills and grievances which make their lives so intolerable. The inability to project such a vision has been one of the chief weaknesses of white radicals in most advanced countries. Confronted with a ruling class which has been able to give workers an increasingly higher standard of living, white radicals have been unable to give workers any vision of a new kind of society which will better meet their concrete material, human, and social needs. Without such a vision, those who are psychologically bent on "revolution for the sake of revolution" begin to dominate the movement, implying that anyone who hesitates to go along with the "baddest" schemes is a "fraidy-cat" and that any attempt to develop a revolutionary perspective, program, and organization is a manifestation of "liberalism."

The present division in the black movement over goals is healthy in the sense that it reflects a growing search for fundamental perspectives and solutions. But the goals projected still reflect the American tendency to "instant revolution." Until the present movement gained its momentum, white power in this country had always been able to keep blacks from serious political struggle over fundamental issues, either by repression or corruption or co-optation of their leaders. Today, the black movement has advanced beyond the stage where it can be indefinitely diverted from serious consideration of what a black revolution in this country must mean.

To solve the immediate and urgent problems of black people, and particularly of black young people, Black Power must revolutionize every institution in modern America: industry, education, health, housing, welfare, transportation. In the next period the black movement will continue to confront the total society with struggles over these issues, no matter how violently white society reacts. In this way the vision of both black and white will be escalated to recognize the general need for revolutionizing these institutions under popular control. Out of this conflict there will begin to emerge the vision of the new society that is now possible in America if politics is put in command of economics.

As long as the black movement does not realize that the solutions to the fundamental ills of this entire society are contained in its struggles, as long as it continues to seek to solve the problems of black people without facing their causes in the society as a whole, it can only dissipate its energies in opportunism, adventurism, and a multiplicity of diverse tendencies and cults. It is true that blacks did not create the problems of this society, but neither did the Vietnamese or Cuban peasants create the problems of Vietnam or Cuba. Blacks will have to assume the leadership to resolve the problems of this society just as the most oppressed people in every country have had to assume this leadership in every modern revolution. No oppressor ever resolved the problems of the oppressed; nor have the oppressed ever been able to deliver themselves from the yoke of oppression until they took upon themselves the responsibility for acquiring the power to do so.

The problem of black people is not just white people. The problem of black people is a structure, a network of institutions created by white people, which has left black people powerless, undeveloped, unfree. That is why the projection of Black Power as the solution to the problems of black people changed the entire character of the movement. Black people were forced to deal with and explore the root-cause of their oppression and to define the meaning of Black Power. From that point onward it was necessary to re-evaluate the past and to plot a new course. As long as the movement was just talking of rights, it was leaving the responsibility for power in the hands of whites. Once the movement began to think in terms of power, the question of what blacks must do with power has been on the agenda.

The launching of the Black Power slogan by SNCC Chairman Stokely Carmichael in 1966 also launched the black movement on a road for which it was totally unprepared theoretically and organizationally. In the course of its struggles to reform the system by actions which challenged the system, SNCC had discovered that black people were powerless and that, being powerless, they could not reform the system. It was an important political discovery coming out of the harsh experiences of real struggles which had made masses of black people and militant activists ready to accept radical concepts.

However, the black movement had not yet established any revolutionary goals for Black Power. SNCC in particular had not done the political analysis of what Black Power meant or of how SNCC itself would have to reorganize if it was to give leadership to the struggle for Black Power. True, three years earlier, at the Grassroots Conference in 1963, Malcolm X had stated that the black revolution, as distinguished from the Negro revolution, had to have a base (land) and had to be achieved by all means necessary, including violence. But this was still a long way from an analysis of revolutionary goals or from a revolutionary program.

As long as the vast majority of black people and black activists were primarily concerned with reforming the system, what had been required from black leaders was chiefly the agitation of the masses by increasing their consciousness of the injustice of the system. The leadership which had emerged during the stage of reform was eminently suited to this task of arousing mass consciousness of grievances.

Black Power requires a different kind of leadership, a leadership that is able to develop the strategy and tactics necessary to organize the masses first to take facets of power and eventually to take total power away from the enemy. To develop such a strategy and tactics, a clear concept of goals is required, because it is only when you have a concept of your goals that you can program a series of struggles toward achieving those goals and measure your progress. At the time of the launching of the Black Power slogan the black movement had not even begun to create this kind of leadership. The result was that the interpretation of Black Power was left entirely to individual spokesmen, the most articulate and charismatic of whom the mass media projected and interpreted to the point that the concept of Black Power was actually being shaped by the tremendous power of the media.

It is easy to blame white power for this take-over of the slogan of Black Power, but it is much more important to understand that it was the movement's unpreparedness which made this take-over possible. Having neglected to make the necessary analysis, the easiest thing for black militants to do was to use Black Power as a slogan to keep the masses in a high state of excitement and expectation. This concept of keeping the masses in a high state of agitation is itself based on the erroneous belief that the masses in themselves are revolutionists, and that if they are constantly urged on by revolutionary rhetoric, they will be able to lead the revolutionary struggle to success. The readiness to believe in the revolutionary spontaneity of the masses was reinforced by the mass urban rebellions which spread throughout the North from 1964 to 1968. These seemed to make the building of a revolutionary organization or the development of revolutionary strategy and tactics superfluous. All that was apparently necessary was a charismatic leader or leaders who could move around the country as mass spokesmen for the long pent-up grievances and the growing black pride and rebellion of the black masses.

With practically every militant black leader seeking to capitalize on this growing black pride and black rebellion, and with the mass media exploiting these militants' hunger for exposure in order to feed its own and the general masses' hunger for star personalities, the organizations which had played the most militant role in the period of reform began to fall apart. This was particularly true of SNCC, from which most was expected because it had already given so much.

As long as SNCC had been engaged in struggle in the South, it had needed some kind of organization. Without an organization, it would have been unable to struggle for a moment since the black masses in the South have few if any democratic illusions, spontaneous struggles by blacks are practically unknown, and no individual spokesmen could long survive the tight conspiracy between the law and the white mob. There are some who say that if SNCC had remained in the South (for example, in Lowndes County), actual political and social conditions would have forced it to develop an organization with the ideology and cadres necessary to lead the struggle for Black Power. This is sheer speculation. Historically, SNCC's major contribution was from 1960 to 1966 in the struggles to translate what had been laid down by law into concrete reality and in the conclusion drawn from these struggles, that integration and democracy in the United States are myths. SNCC came to this conclusion from its experiences in the South at the point when the black masses in the North had begun to rebel spontaneously. It moved immediately to give leadership to these masses without realizing that spontaneous rebellion is not revolution but rather represents the highest stage of the frustration of the masses seeking a way out from intolerable oppression.

SNCC was by no means the only black organization to capitalize on the spontaneous rebellion of the masses. All over the country individual leaders and groups emerged to make demands on the power structure, threatening it with continuing mass rebellion unless it acceded to certain demands, and claiming to have the power to turn this rebellion on or off. The result has been increasing corruption and growing opportunism in the black movement as individual militants compete with each other as the "real" spokesmen for the black community in order to obtain grants and positions for themselves and their associates. Thus the rebellion of the masses has been exploited to advance individuals.

When SNCC was unable to provide the revolutionary leadership and organization needed in the struggle for Black Power, a vacuum was created in the black movement which was soon to be filled by the Black Panther Party. Particularly after the murder of Dr. King in April 1968, the Black Panther Party began to reflect the mushrooming revolutionary force of black school and street youth seeking a political identity, national leadership, and militant action. This social force had already been growing by leaps and bounds in the wake of the urban rebellions. The King murder shook up every black organization, every black grouping, every section of the black community, but its greatest impact was on these youth, particularly those of junior and senior high school age. As of April 4, 1968, every white administration, every white institution, had lost its legitimacy, its validity, and its authority in the eyes of these youth. They were now "ready for anything."

Black street youth have certain political characteristics which reveal the high stage of revolutionary consciousness that has already been achieved by America's "rebels with a cause":

1. Unlike the black middle classes who dream of building black economic and political power with the support and encouragement of the white power structure, these youth see themselves as engaged in continuing confrontation and irreconcilable struggle with the police, the school system, industry, the unions, the housing authorities, health and welfare administrators —indeed, with every institution inside the black community.

2. Their consciousness springs from very concrete grievances, the everyday abuses and hardships suffered by the great bulk of the black community on the job, in the streets, in the schools, at the welfare office, in the hospitals; grievances with which their elders have learned to live but which these young people refuse to tolerate any longer. Their refusal to accommodate themselves to oppression has, in turn, made them the victims of even more open and vicious oppression than that suffered by their elders.

3. They also recognize that although a particular confrontation may be precipitated by an individual incident, their struggle is not against just one or another individual but against a whole power structure comprising a complex network of politicians, university and school administrators, landlords, merchants, usurers, realtors, insurance personnel, contractors, union leaders, licensing and inspection bureaucrats, racketeers, lawyers, and especially policemen—the overwhelming majority of whom are both white and absentee, and who exploit the black ghetto in much the same way that Western powers exploit the colonies and neo-colonies in Africa, Asia, and Latin America.

4. They are for the most part anti-capitalist, generally believing that the profit system is at the root of black oppression and that as long as capitalism exists black people will become increasingly expendable.

5. They are also consciously anti-imperialist, identifying with the world black revolution, opposed to United States exploitation of the colored peoples of Africa, Asia, and Latin America, and determined not to die abroad for a democracy denied them at home.

6. They are consciously anti-liberal. Having assimilated the experiences of the civil rights movement, they recognize the futility of reform legislation and are ready to pursue the struggle by all means necessary, by which they usually mean armed struggle. To an extent difficult for most whites to understand, their fundamental attitudes to life and struggle have been shaped by their own daily battles to survive on the city streets and more recently, by the violent deaths of Malcolm, Martin Luther King Jr., and more than two dozen Black Panthers.

These attitudes, taken as a whole, amount to a repudiation not only of the American racist-capitalist system and American politics but also of the vehement anti-communism or anti-egalitarianism which is deeply rooted in white Americans. The average white American's profound antagonism to communism stems essentially from the benefits which the great majority of whites have received from the American way of life as a system of social mobility for the individual and for successive ethnic groups. For the average black street youth, this concept of America as a land of opportunity and peaceful progress is not only a fraud but an insult. The final proof that the American Dream was dead was the vicious murder of the man who had tried hardest to make it live—Dr. Martin Luther King Jr.

The Black Panther Party represents the first major attempt by a section of the black movement to form a revolutionary vanguard party based on this growing revolutionary social force. But it is by no means the last. Because it was the first, it has inevitably made some mistakes, and careful study and evaluation can teach the movement many important lessons for the future. To evaluate the Black Panther Party is not to question the sincerity and revolutionary dedication of its members, about which there can be no question. But the party is a political party, and it must therefore be judged politically in terms of whether or not it adequately meets the requirements of a revolutionary vanguard party.

In the first place, the fanfare with which the party announced its existence and intentions reveals democratic illusions about the rights a revolutionary party seriously contending for power can expect to enjoy in this country. Secondly, the original name of the party, the Black Panther Party for Self-Defense, shows that its central focus is confrontation with, reaction to, and defense against white oppression, particularly in the form of the police occupation army, rather than an offensive strategy leading to the conquest of power. Its Ten-Point Program, which is supposed to contain such a strategy, is more a statement of grievances and concessions demanded from the white power structure than it is a program to mobilize black people in escalating struggles for control and power.

In developing a program to mobilize black people in revolutionary struggles to gain control and power, three things must be borne in mind:

1. The struggle is a struggle to defeat those in power and to gain power for one's own forces. It is a power struggle to get rid of one power and replace it with another. Such a goal cannot be achieved overnight or by instant revolution. The struggle must be a protracted one, taking advantage of the enemy's internal contradictions and finding ways to use his strength against him rather than confronting him head-on.

2. The people who are striving for power must themselves be transformed into new people in the course of the struggle. Their will to struggle, their vision of what they are struggling for, their social consciousness and responsibility, and their capacity to govern must all be systematically increased. The struggle must therefore be an escalating one, focused on problems the people can learn from. It cannot be hit-and-miss or in reaction to what the enemy does, but must be based on a strategy which has been mapped out in advance and which permits the organization to take advantage of the enemy's predictable actions or mistakes. Indispensable to victory is the strategic employment of time as a dimension of struggle within which contradictions are deepened, conflicts escalate, and there is an accelerated growth of the revolutionary social forces, not only in numbers and understanding but in organization and sense of community. In the wake of the spontaneous mass rebellions from 1964-1968, each of the erupting communities experienced temporarily that sense of community

and mutual responsibility which is characteristic of most Southern black communities but which has been subverted by the dog-eat-dog existence of the cities. Spontaneous rebellions alone cannot give this sense of community and underlying social structure which city dwellers so urgently need. This can only come from developing struggles.

3. All struggles must take place over very concrete issues and institutions whose resolution and control the people feel are vital to their existence.

The black community has all the necessary ingredients for such programs of struggle in every institution inside the black community. Black people already know that these institutions have failed them and that they have a right to take over their control. By giving leadership to programs of struggle to achieve control over each of these institutions, a black revolutionary party can develop united front organizations within each institution which would be *de facto* parallel power structures. The more these institutions inside the black community become liberated from white control and reorganized to meet the needs of black people, the more they become *bases* for expanded struggle, since the community would be prepared to defend them by all means necessary. Thus, the black movement can expand from programs of struggle for control of the black community into programs of struggle to control the cities, and thence to national struggles.

Lacking such programs of struggle to develop the urban equivalent of liberated areas, the Black Panther Party has resorted to social service programs, such as the Free Breakfast and Free Health programs. Instead of mobilizing the black community to compel the city, state, or federal government to provide such services under community control, the party has taken over the responsibility for their funding and administration.

Still caught up in the illusion that the masses are revolutionary in themselves, the Black Panther Party has grown at the rate of a small mass party rather than that of a revolutionary vanguard party. A vanguard party recruits into membership *only* those who have previously undergone rigorous orientation training and tests to determine fitness for membership. A small mass party, on the other hand, tends to recruit into membership those who are followers—those who are sympathetic to its aims and attracted by its image but who have not met strict standards of membership. As a result, the small mass party finds itself being led by those who should be following.

The Black Panther Party has developed other weaknesses. In reacting against the non-violent philosophy and opportunism of many black organizations, it has been easy to veer over into a philosophy of violence and an adventurism which, despite its aggressive appearance, actually keeps the organization tied up in legal defense actions. Critical of the lack of ideology in such organizations as SNCC and CORE, the Panthers borrowed intact the *Little Red Book,* without distinguishing between what is appropriate to China, or a post-revolutionary situation, and what is appropriate to the United States, or a pre-revolutionary situation. Repelled by the intellectualism of most SNCC members, the Party's appeal has been almost exclusively to black street youth who, in the absence of a highly developed political leadership and programming, naturally tend to impatience and a militaristic viewpoint. Forced on the defensive by the "search and destroy" operations of the police, the Party has been led, step by step, into increased reliance upon the financial and legal help of white radicals, as well as into variations on their outmoded ideas of class struggle and "black and white, unite and fight."

Despite these mistakes and weaknesses, the Black Panther Party is historically important because it has demonstrated conclusively the tremendous potential among black street youth in this country for the discipline and self-sacrifice necessary to overthrow racism and capitalism, and the tremendous hunger for a total ideology which will invest their lives with social and historical meaning and direct their explosive energies into revolutionary political channels. It is this potential and this hunger—far more than any immediate danger from actual actions or rhetoric—which has provoked the counterattack from the police. In turn, the ruthlessness of the counterattack has clarified for many black adults the manner in which racism in this country operates to deprive black youth of the right to live and learn from experience. The rallying of the entire black community to the defense of the Black Panthers is an indication of the essential unity that exists among blacks of all ages and generations in the face of white oppression, a source of strength whose implications have yet to be fully developed.

"What we need is leadership." This is and has long been the cry of black people searching for a road out from their oppression in white America. When blacks speak of leaders, they are usually thinking of a man like Martin Luther King, who articulated their dreams, or Malcolm, who had the unique ability to challenge and chide black people at the same time, or Stokely, who made blacks glow with black pride, or H. Rap Brown, who made clear the readiness of black youth to make their extermination too expensive for the white man even to contemplate.

Each of these leaders has made a major contribution to the developing momentum of the black revolution. Each both expressed and helped to create a certain stage of the movement. Each was a public figure, attacking the enemy openly and frontally. Malcolm was murdered on a public platform as he was making clear his intention to organize ties between the black revolutions at home and abroad. King was murdered after he began to take an active part in the anti-Vietnam movement, threatening to meddle in the arena of foreign policy that white power considers its own preserve and in which it felt on very shaky ground. Now Fred Hampton, who was emerging as a black street youth leader, has been ambushed in his bed.

These murders should give the black movement much food for thought. The question is not that death is to be feared, but rather whether a movement which has reached the stage of contending for power has the right to organize itself in such a way that its leadership is so much in front. Lenin went into hiding many times—without announcing that he was about to do so. Ho Chi Minh changed his identity so often that there was frequent speculation as to whether he was still alive. One cannot imagine a Vietcong fighter marching into Saigon with "Guerrilla Fighter" or "Minister of Defense" inscribed on his jacket. Yet so pervasive is the theatrical model of revolution that those supposedly struggling for power have been publicly playing the roles and assuming the posts of those who have already achieved the power to defend themselves.

As long as the black movement and black people were seeking primarily to reform the system, what was required from leadership was relatively simple. It was the outspoken, unrelenting condemnation of the system, arousing the black masses to a heightened sense of their grievances. This is something that black leaders have always done well. The chief difference has been that in this period they have had organizations behind them and have been part of an ongoing national movement. When the movement changed from being essentially an attempt to reform the system into a struggle for power, a new phase began. This new phase requires a different kind of organization, with a different, more scientific, ideology; different, more disciplined, members; a different, more functional, structure; a different, more strategically developed, program of struggle; and a different, less flamboyant leadership.

What has bogged the movement down during the last few years is that it has wanted to change direction without changing the tasks, the structure, and the activities of leadership. The old leaders, accustomed to the limelight, have wanted to keep their image public. They have been unable to adapt themselves to the new need for the painstaking and often unglamorous tasks of building cadres who are dedicated to working in the community, carrying out and developing programs of struggle that will lead to the conquest of power, and projecting political solutions and perspectives of power to which the masses may not immediately subscribe but which they can begin to understand through a process of escalating struggle. Considering how the movement actually developed (i.e., empirically), it is natural that the black masses continue to look for charismatic leaders who can articulate their grievances and put up a tough public image, and that leaders continue to come forward to play this role. But those who have recognized the seriousness of the struggle for power and the kind of strategy and tactics, leadership and organization, required for such a struggle have no right to confuse what the masses *want* with what the movement *needs*. If they have any doubt, they have only to reflect for a moment on how little we know about the counter-revolution, its leaders, its cadres, even its numbers. Yet it is common knowledge that its forces are far better organized, better disciplined, and better equipped than those of the black movement.

As long as the black movement does not set itself the task of creating the kind of leadership necessary for a serious struggle for power, it will betray the fact that it is still expecting white power to resolve the problems of black people. Blacks will still be evading the struggle for power and the responsibilities that go with such a struggle.

When the perspective of blacks revolutionizing and ruling America is projected as the only solution to the total crisis of this society, the first response from black and white is usually negative. This stems, first of all, from the acceptance of the myth of "majority rule"—as if this country were not ruled by a minority of individuals and corporations. Also, both black and white are still stuck in the statistical picture of blacks as a small minority, when in politics what matters is not numbers as such but rather the strategic position of your forces. Even from the point of view of numbers, colored people constitute approximately 25 percent of the American population when you take into consideration the Third World peoples inside the United States, all of whom have suffered a similar exploitation under the American racist-capitalist system.

The chief objection whites have to Black Revolutionary Power is basically racist: they simply cannot conceive of blacks ever having the political intelligence or skill to govern. Even those few whites who accept Black Power in theory are fearful that the deep racial animosity which exists in the average white American would mean such unceasing and bloody white resistance that blacks would never have a chance to rule.

Blacks also still lack confidence in their capacity to rule. Moreover, having experienced the barbarism of white racism for so many centuries and conscious of being outnumbered, they can't even imagine a situation in which they are ruling whites. Hence, when they talk about Black Power or the black revolution, they are usually envisaging either complete geographical separation from whites; *or* control of only the black community, leaving revolution in the "mother country" to whites; *or* eventually being the junior partner in a revolutionary coalition led by whites.

What all these objections and hesitations show is a lack of understanding of the nature of all revolutions and of the specific character of the American Revolution. In any revolution the new ruling power derives its legitimacy not only from the benefits which it brings to the specific social forces which it represents, but from the fact that it replaces the old system with a new one that benefits all the people in the country. The great need of the total community in the United States is a rapid development in all the people of a social consciousness, a sense of social responsibility, and a control over economic and social institutions, all of which are necessary for self-government. This is the revolutionary humanist essence of the revolutions now taking place in Asia, Latin America, and the liberated areas of Africa. It is also the essence of the black revolution in America.

Blacks are the social force with the greatest need to struggle for control over the economic and social institutions which dominate their daily lives because they are the ones these institutions have most manifestly failed. In the course of the protracted struggles necessary to achieve this control, blacks will be the ones who can most rapidly develop the parallel power structures and the skills to govern these institutions on new foundations. They are the ones with the greatest need to redefine the goals and methods of these institutions to make them relevant to human rather than economic needs.

A new revolutionary power also derives its legitimacy from the fact that it is the only social force which can put an end to the prevailing disorder and create a new order in which new social disciplines have been born out of a new faith in the potentialities of man. Today the accumulation of social problems and of violence and counter-violence in the United States is reaching the point where there appears to be no possibility of peaceful coexistence between the races, the nations, the sexes, and the generations. Human life itself is beginning to seem less valuable than that of animals. As I wrote in the *Manifesto for a Black Revolutionary Party*: "Concretely, American society faces only three real alternatives: 1) to continue rotting away as it is today; 2) naked counter-revolution; 3) Black Revolutionary Power. The fact that these are the only concrete alternatives makes Black Revolutionary Power as realistic a possibility as the other two."

As we enter the 1970's, time is running out on the first alternative. The second alternative, fascism or the "new order" which enforces adherence to the *old* values by violence and intimidation, is coming closer every day. Experience shows that fascism cannot be stopped short of a total revolution which establishes a new social order based on new values. The struggle *by blacks* to establish this new social order and *between whites* to determine how far they are ready to go to support or crush this new social order will dominate the 1970's.

*1970*

## Selected Modern Reader Paperbacks

# MONTHLY REVIEW

## an independent socialist magazine
## edited by Paul M. Sweezy and Harry Magdoff

*Business Week:* ". . . a brand of socialism that is thorough-going and tough-minded, drastic enough to provide the sharp break with the past that many left-wingers in the underdeveloped countries see as essential. At the same time they maintain a sturdy independence of both Moscow and Peking that appeals to neutralists. And their skill in manipulating the abstruse concepts of modern economics impresses would-be intellectuals. . . . Their analysis of the troubles of capitalism is just plausible enough to be disturbing."

*Bertrand Russell:* "Your journal has been of the greatest interest to me over a period of time. I am not a Marxist by any means as I have sought to show in critiques published in several books, but I recognize the power of much of your own analysis and where I disagree I find your journal valuable and of stimulating importance. I want to thank you for your work and to tell you of my appreciation of it."

*The Wellesley Department of Economics:* " . . . the leading Marxist intellectual (not Communist) economic journal published anywhere in the world, and is on our subscription list at the College library for good reasons."

*Albert Einstein:* "Clarity about the aims and problems of socialism is of greatest significance in our age of transition. . . . I consider the founding of this magazine to be an important public service." (In his article, "Why Socialism" in Vol. I, No. 1.)

DOMESTIC: $7 for one year, $12 for two years, $5 for one-year student subscription.

FOREIGN: $8 for one year, $14 for two years, $6 for one-year student subscription. (Subscription rates subject to change.)

116 West 14th Street, New York, New York 10011